Ninja Foodi XL Pro Air Oven Complete Cookbook 2021

1000-Days Delicious & Step-By-Step Homemade Recipes for All the Family and Friends

Gladys Mullins

Contents

Introduction 5

Basic of Ninja Foodi XL Pro Air Fry Oven 5

Guide to Quick Using Ninja Foodi XL Pro

Air Fry Oven 6

Chapter 1: Breakfast Recipes 7

Perfect Cinnamon Toast 7

French toast Sticks 8

Delicious Egg and Cheese Muffins 9

French toast Bread Pudding 10

Breakfast Frittata Recipe 11

Breakfast Soufflé 12

Avocado Eggs 13

Cereal French toast 14

Breakfast Oats 15

Breakfast Hash 16

Chapter 2: Snacks and Appetizers Recipes
.... 17

Baked Apples 17

Beef Jerky 18

Crispy Potatoes with Mayo 19

Brussels Sprouts With Bacon 20

Baked Loaded Potatoes 21

Zucchini Crisps 22

Blue Cheese Chicken Wings 23

Jalapeno Poppers 24

French Fries 25

Mixed Nuts 26

Chapter 3: Chicken & Poultry Recipes 27

Chicken Stir Fry 27

Roasted Chicken with Apple 28

Yogurt Chicken 29

Buffalo wings 30

BBQ Chicken Wings 31

Cajun Spice Chicken 32

Honey Sriracha Lime Chicken Wings ... 33

Spice-Rubbed Chicken Breasts with

Chimichurri 34

Teriyaki Glazed Chicken 35

Tarragon-Mustard Chicken 36

Whole Chicken Roast 37

Cheesy Chicken 38

Chicken Tikka Masala 39

Turkey in Ninja Oven 40

Country Style Chicken Wings 41

Chicken Meat Patties 42

Chapter 4: Fish & Seafood Recipes 43

Lobster Tail Casserole 43

Haddock Cream Casserole 44

White Fish with Lemon Pepper 45

Garlic Parmesan Shrimp 46

Baked Shrimp with Garlic Sauce 47

Dill Seafood Paella 48

Seafood Mushrooms Casserole 49

Halibut Scallops Bake 50

Breaded Shrimp 51

Chapter 5: Beef, Pork, and Lamb **52**

Lamb Chops with Garlic Sauce 52

Beef Potato Medley 53

Pork Chops with Broccoli 54

Russian Beef 55

Breaded Pork Chops 56

Roast Lamb with Potatoes 57

Spiced Pork Chops 58

Lamb Leg with Mint Sauce 59

Garlicky Pork Chops 60

Chapter 6: Interesting Recipes **61**

Blooming Onion 61

Chicken Enchiladas 62

Baked Potatoes 63

Whole Turkey with Gravy 64

Fiesta Chicken Casserole 65

Thanksgiving Turkey 66

Chicken Casserole 67

Hash brown casserole 68

Ground Beef Casserole 69

Air Fried Pizza 70

Chicken Sheet Bake 71

Meatball Casserole 72

Turkey breast 73

Roasted Chicken 74

Chapter 7: Vegetables and Sides **75**

Vegetables Mix 75

Brussels Sprouts Gratin 76

Mayo Broccoli Casserole 77

Green Bean Casserole 78

Vegetable Casserole 79

Mushroom Skewers 80

Sweet Potato Casserole 81

Cauliflower Broccoli Medley 82

Italian Baked Vegetables 83

Chapter 8: Dessert Recipes **84**

Chocolate Cake 84

Strawberry Roll Cake 85

Fudgy Brownies 86

Cherry Eggrolls 86

Pear Pies 88

Cherry Crumble 89

Pecan Apples 90

Apple Pies 91

Butter Cake 92

Conclusion **93**

Introduction

Today, finding a multipurpose cooking unit is not that of a challenge; rather, finding a perfect one for your kitchen requires a bit of a struggle, as there are unlimited options available. One brand that has earned our confidence in this regard is Ninja Foodi. Not only has the brand launched series of cooking appliances, but it keeps raising the bars by bringing new ideas to the market. The Ninja Foodi XL pro Air Fry Oven is one such innovation that has taken over the food-tech world with its amazing cooking features, a smart design, the XL size, and a multilayer cooking system. This 10-in-1 multipurpose kitchen miracle is capable of providing a variety of cooking options all in a single device. With its efficient electric heating system, now you can bake, roast, Air fry, broil and dehydrate all types of food in no time.

Basic of Ninja Foodi XL Pro Air Fry Oven

After the successful launch of its series of Air Fryer and Air Fry Ovens, Ninja Foodi has come up with its XL Pro Air Fry Oven to meet the needs of those who want to cook large servings sizes, whole turkeys, or chicken in their electric oven while trying different modes of cooking at one place.

• True Surround Convection: Up to 10X the convection power vs. a traditional full-size convection oven for faster, crispier, and juicy results
• Ultimate Versatility: Air Fry, Air Roast, Bake, Whole Roast, Broil, Toast, Bagel, Dehydrate, Reheat, and Pizza, all in one powerful 1800-watt appliance
• Quick Family Meals: 90-second oven preheat time and up to 30% faster cooking than a traditional full-size convection oven
• Extra-Large Countertop Oven Capacity: 2-level even cooking, no rotating required—fit a 5-lb chicken and a sheet pan of vegetables, 2 12-in pizzas, or a 12-lb turkey
• Air Fryer Healthy Meals: Up to 75% less fat when using the Air Fry function vs. traditional deep frying(tested against hand-cut, deep-fried French fries)
• Digital Display Handle: The optimal oven rack positions will illuminate based on the selected function. When the door is open, display settings freeze to prevent any accidental changes to the cook cycle.
• Crispier Results: Up to 30% crispier results vs. a traditional convection oven
• Perfect Countertop Oven for Baking: Up to 50% more even baking results vs. a leading countertop oven
• Easy Meals for Large Groups: Make 2 sheet pan meals at once for entertaining or weekly meal prep
• Includes 2 sheet pans, 2 wire racks, air fry basket, roast tray, crumb tray

Guide to Quick Using Ninja Foodi XL Pro Air Fry Oven

If you are a newbie or you are setting your hands on this appliance for the first time, then here is how you can cook using its different cooking functions:

1. First, plug in the Ninja Foodi XL pro Air Fry Oven and switch it ON. The led display will be lit up, indicating that the device is working.

2. Since this Ninja XL pro Air Fry Oven quickly preheats, you need to prepare the food first and keep it ready for cooking before preheating.

3. Place the Drip or crumb tray inside, at the bottom of the oven to protect its base from food particle and grease.

4. Use the Air fryer basket, baking pan, roasting pan, or any other suitable accessory to place the food inside according to the instructions of a particular recipe.

5. You can insert trays into any portion of this air fry oven to accommodate your food in four layers if needed and select the RACK LAYER option 1,2,3,4 from the control panel according to your need.

6. When the food is ready, you can preheat the appliance. Close its door and select the desired cooking operation: Bake, Whole roast, Air Roast, Air Broil, Air Fry, Dehydrate, pizza, toast, bagel, or Reheat.

7. By selecting this program, the device will show the preset temperature and cooking time on the display; you can change it by using the "+" or "- "keys for temperature and time to increase or decrease the values, respectively.

8. If you are toasting bread or bagels, then use the temp and time keys to adjust the desired darkness of the toasts and the number of slices. The machine will automatically adjust the cooking temperature and time according to the desired darkness and set slices.

9. Press the start button to initiate preheating. The display timer does not start ticking until the appliance is preheated. When it reaches the desired temperature, the display will show"FOOD" and beep to show if the device is preheated.

10. Place the prepared food inside and close the lid to initiate cooking.

11. Once the cooking function is completed, the device will beep to indicate that the food is now ready to serve.

Chapter 1: Breakfast Recipes

Perfect Cinnamon Toast

Prep Time: 10 Minutes | Cook Time: 5 Minutes | Makes: 2 Servings

Ingredients:

- 4 slices of whole wheat bread
- 4 tablespoons of salted butter, at room temperature
- 4 tablespoons of brown sugar, or to taste
- ½ teaspoon of cinnamon, ground
- ½ teaspoon of vanilla extract
- Pinch of salt

Preparation:

1. Select BAKE function of Ninja Foodi XL Pro Air Oven by adjusting the temperature to 400 degrees F and set time to 7 minutes.

2. Press start so the preheating begins.

3. In a bowl mix butter with sugar, cinnamon, and vanilla.

4. Add a pinch of salt as well.

5. Spread this mixture equally over the bread slices.

6. Put the coated bread slices on a sheet pan and place it inside Ninja Foodi XL Pro Air Oven.

7. Bake at 400 degrees F for 5 minutes.

8. Remove it from Ninja Foodi XL Pro Air Oven and serve.

Serving Suggestion: Serve the toast with peanut butter or almond butter

Variation Tip: Any bread variation can be used.

Nutritional Information per Serving: Calories 395 | Fat 24g | Sodium 506mg | Carbs 36.6g | Fiber 4g | Sugar 15.7g | Protein 7.5g

French toast Sticks

Prep Time: 10 Minutes| Cook Time: 12 Minutes| Makes: 3 Servings

Ingredients:

- 3 organic eggs
- 1/3 cup milk
- 1/3 teaspoon vanilla extract
- 1/3 teaspoon ground cinnamon
- 1/2 cup sugar, granulated
- 6 slices white bread, cut in thirds
- Oil spray, for greasing
- ½ cup Maple syrup, as needed

Preparation:

1. Take a bowl and whisk eggs in it.

2. Then pour in the milk along with cinnamon and vanilla extract.

3. Then add sugar and whisk all the ingredients well.

4. Take an air fryer basket and grease it with oil spray.

5. Dip the bread pieces into the egg mixture and then transfer it to the air fryer basket.

6. Select start and preheat the Ninja Foodi XL Pro Air Oven at 400 degrees F for 12 minutes.

7. Once preheating done, Air fry the bread for 7 minutes, then press Start/pause to stop the Ninja Foodi XL Pro Air Oven.

8. Turn the bread and then again Air fry for 5 more minutes.

9. Once the cooking is complete, remove the basket and then drizzle maple syrup on top of toast.

10. Serve as a delicious breakfast.

Serving Suggestion: Serve the sticks with peanut butter

Variation Tip: Use brown sugar for change of flavor

Nutritional Information per Serving: Calories 390 | Fat 5.9g | Sodium 202mg | Carbs 79g | Fiber 0g | Sugar 67g | Protein 8g

Delicious Egg and Cheese Muffins

Prep Time: 15 Minutes| Cook Time: 7 Minutes| Makes: 2 Servings

Ingredients:

- 2 small organic eggs, whisked
- 2 tablespoons olive oil
- 75 ml of milk
- 100 grams of gluten-free flour
- 1 tablespoon baking powder
- ½ teaspoon of mustard powder
- 4 ounces of Parmesan, grated
- 1/4 teaspoon Worcestershire sauce
- Salt and black pepper, to taste

Equipment

- 8 paper muffin cases

Preparation:

1. Preheat the Ninja Foodi XL Pro Air Oven at 400 degrees F for 20 minutes.
2. Take 8 muffin cases and double up to make it 4 cups.
3. Take a bowl and whisk the eggs with olive oil and milk.
4. Then add the plain flour, mustard powder, baking powder, salt, black pepper, Worcestershire sauce, and Parmesan cheese.
5. Mix all the ingredients well.
6. Pour equal divided batter among 4 muffin cups.
7. Put the muffin cups on the baking tray.
8. Place it inside the Ninja Foodi XL Pro Air Oven, and close the lid.
9. Bake it for 5-7 minutes.
10. Once egg muffins are cooked, serve and enjoy.

Serving Suggestion: Serve it with cream cheese

Variation Tip: you can skip mustard powder if not like it.

Nutritional Information per Serving: Calories 565 | Fat 31g | Sodium 760mg | Carbs 48 g | Fiber 5g | Sugar 4g | Protein 27g

French toast Bread Pudding

Prep Time: 15 Minutes| Cook Time: 45 Minutes| Makes: 2 Servings

Ingredients:

- 6 eggs, organic
- 3/4 cup heavy cream
- 2 tablespoons sugar
- 1 teaspoon orange liqueur
- Salt, to taste
- 2 cinnamon buns, broken in pieces
- 1/3 cup dried cherries

Directions

1. Take a bowl and whisk eggs in it.
2. Then add heavy cream, sugar, and mix well.
3. Then add orange liqueur, cherries, and salt.
4. Mix the ingredients for fine incorporation.
5. Now dredge the buns in the egg mixture.
6. Cover the bowl and refrigerate for 20 minutes.
7. Preheat the Ninja Foodi XL Pro Air Oven by select roasting for 3 minutes at 400 degrees.
8. Pour the refrigerated mixture into the ramekins.
9. Cover it with aluminum foil.
10. Put ramekins inside the oven.
11. Select ROAST, and adjust the temperature to 325 degrees F for 45 minutes.
12. Once the cooking cycle completely take out the pudding and serve.

Serving Suggestion: Serve it with cream cheese

Variation Tip: you can use any other flavored liquor of your choice

Nutritional Information per Serving: Calories 581 | Fat 31g | Sodium 321mg | Carbs 55g | Fiber 1.7g | Sugar 37g | Protein 18 g

Breakfast Frittata Recipe

Prep Time: 10 Minutes| Cook Time: 13 Minutes| Makes: 4 Servings

Ingredients:

- 4-5 large organic eggs
- 2 Italian sausages, chopped
- 2 cherry tomatoes, chopped
- Oil spray, for greasing
- 1/4 cup of parsley, chopped
- 1/2 cup of Parmesan cheese, per liking
- Salt and Black Pepper, to taste

Preparation:

1. The first step is to preheat the Ninja Foodi XL Pro Air Oven at 365 degrees F for 5 minutes

2. Use the baking pan of Ninja Foodi XL Pro Air Oven and add cherry tomatoes, and sausage to it.

3. Grease the ingredients with oil spray.

4. Place the pan in Ninja Foodi XL Pro Air Oven and cook it for 5 minutes.

5. Meanwhile, whisk the egg in a bowl and add parmesan cheese, parsley, salt, and pepper in it.

6. Take out the baking pan and transfer the ingredient to the egg mixture.

7. Bake in the oven for 8 minutes at 350 degrees F.

8. Once the eggs get firm, serve and enjoy.

Serving Suggestion: Serve with roasted potatoes

Variation Tip: Use cheese according to personal preference

Nutritional Information per Serving: Calories 371| Fat 29g | Sodium 748mg | Carbs 4g | Fiber 0g | Sugar 2g | Protein 21g

Breakfast Soufflé

Prep Time: 10 Minutes| Cook Time: 25 Minutes| Makes: 4 Servings

Ingredients:

- 1/2 cup all-purpose flour
- 1/2 cup butter
- 1-1/4 cup almond milk
- ½ cup brown sugar
- 4 egg yolks
- 1 teaspoon vanilla extract
- ½ ounce of white sugar
- 1 teaspoon of cream of tartar
- Oil spray, for greasing

Preparation:

1. First press the start/pause button and turn on Ninja Foodi XL Pro Air Oven and set temperatures to 350 degrees F for 5 minutes.

2. Take a bowl and mix butter with flour.

3. In a saucepan pour milk and sugar and let it simmer over medium flame.

4. Then add flour mixture to the milk.

5. Cook it for 6 minutes and then let it get cool.

6. Next, grease the soufflé dishes with oil spray.

7. In a large mixing bowl whisk egg yolks, white sugar, vanilla extract and cream of tartar, and Pour this mixture into a soufflé dish and top it with a flour milk mixture.

8. Put the soufflé dish in the Ninja Foodi XL Pro Air Oven and then bake it for 18 minutes.

9. Once done, serve and enjoy.

Serving Suggestion: Serve with berries topping

Variation Tip: use dairy milk instead of almond milk

Nutritional Information per Serving: Calories 539 | Fat 42g | Sodium 187mg | Carbs 37g | Fiber 2g | Sugar 23g | Protein 5g

Avocado Eggs

Prep Time: 10 Minutes| Cook Time: 10 Minutes| Makes: 2 Servings

Ingredients:

- 1 avocado, pitted
- 2 large eggs organic
- Salt and black pepper, to taste
- 2 bacon slices, cooked and chopped

Preparation:

1. Take an avocado and cut it in half.

2. Scoop some flesh out from the center.

3. Crack one egg in the center of the avocado and season it with salt and black pepper.

4. Place the egg into the baking tray.

5. Turn on the air roast function of Ninja Foodi XL Pro Air Oven by pressing the air roast mode.

6. Set time to 10 minutes at 375 degrees F.

7. Press the start, and when the timer beep put the tray inside the oven.

8. Once the cooking cycle complete, take out and serve with a sprinkle of bacon bits.

Serving Suggestion: Serve with slices of bread

Variation Tip: You can use turkey bacon to lower the calories

Nutritional Information per Serving: Calories 325 | Fat 27g| Sodium 478mg | Carbs 9 g | Fiber 6g | Sugar 0.7g | Protein 12.1g

Cereal French toast

Prep Time: 15 Minutes | Cook Time: 20 Minutes | Makes: 6 Servings

Ingredients:

- 14 ounces of coconut milk, sweetened
- 4 organic eggs
- ¼ teaspoon cinnamon
- 6 cups flake cereal, sugar-coated
- 6 slices brioche bread slices
- Cooking spray, for greasing
- ½ cup Maple syrup, for serving

Preparation:

1. Take a bowl and whisk eggs in it.
2. Then add coconut milk and cinnamon.
3. Now place cereal in a plastic bag and crush using a hand.
4. Add it to a shallow bowl.
5. Dip the bread in the milk then dredge in cereal.
6. Repeat the step for all bread slices.
7. Select the AIR Fry mode of Ninja Foodi XL Pro Air Oven and set the temperature to 425°F, for 15-20 minutes.
8. Press START to begin preheating.
9. Now oil sprays the Ninja Sheet Pan and places bread slices on it.
10. Air fry it in Ninja Foodi XL Pro Air Oven for 20 minutes
11. Remember to flip halfway through.
12. Once cooking is done, remove and serve with drizzle of maple syrup.

Serving Suggestion: Serve the toast with jam

Variation Tip: Use nutmeg instead of cinnamon for change of flavor

Nutritional Information per Serving: Calories 634 | Fat20.9 g |Sodium 582mg | Carbs 92.2 g| Fiber 4.2g | Sugar 55g | Protein 15.2g

Breakfast Oats

Prep Time: 10 Minutes| Cook Time: 17 Minutes| Makes: 2 Servings

Ingredients:

- 1 cup steel-cut oats
- 2 cups of coconut milk
- 1 apple, peeled and chopped
- 2 tablespoons of brown sugar
- ½ teaspoon of cinnamon

Preparation:

1. Combine all the listed ingredients in a baking dish and mix well.

2. Place it inside Ninja Foodi XL Pro Air Oven and bake for 17 minutes at 360 degrees F.

3. Serve it as a hearty breakfast.

Serving Suggestion: Serve with mixed berries

Variation Tip: You can use dairy milk instead of coconut milk

Nutritional Information per Serving: Calories 726 | Fat 58g | Sodium 40mg | Carbs 51g | Fiber 10g | Sugar 28 g | Protein 8.8g

Breakfast Hash

Prep Time: 10 Minutes | Cook Time: 20 Minutes | Makes: 6 Servings

Ingredients:

- 1-1/2 cups russet potatoes, peeled and cubed
- 2 kielbasa sausages, cubed
- 2 small yellow onions, peeled and chopped
- 1/3 cup carrots
- ¼ cup green beans
- 1/3 cup corn
- ¼ cup unsalted butter, melted
- 1 teaspoon paprika
- Salt and black pepper, to taste

Preparation:

1. Take a large bowl and add onion, potatoes, kielbasa, and all the vegetables, then pour in the melted butter to it.

2. Add salt, paprika, and black pepper.

3. Toss all the ingredients well.

4. Select BAKE function of Ninja Foodi XL Pro Air Oven by adjusting the temperature to 400 degrees F and set time to 20 minutes.

5. Press start so the preheating begins.

6. Transfer the ingredients to a ninja foodie sheet pan and bake it in Ninja Foodi XL Pro Air Oven until the cooking cycle completes.

7. Remember to shake the ingredient after 10 minutes.

8. Once done, serve and enjoy.

Serving Suggestion: Serve the hash with ketchup

Variation Tip: Sweet potatoes can be used as well

Nutritional Information per Serving: Calories 353 | Fat 29g | Sodium 726mg | Carbs10g | Fiber 1.8g | Sugar 2.1g | Protein 11g

Chapter 2: Snacks and Appetizers Recipes

Baked Apples

Prep Time: 15 Minutes| Cook Time: 45 Minutes| Makes: 2 Servings

Ingredients:

- 2 gala apples, skin remove and cut in half
- 1 lemon, juice only
- 6 teaspoons light brown sugar
- 1/2 stick butter, cut into 16 pieces
- 10 teaspoons granulated sugar

TOPPINGS Ingredients:

- 2 scoops Vanilla ice cream
- 2 tablespoons caramel syrup
- 2 tablespoons peanuts, chopped
- 6 vanilla wafers

Preparation:

1. Pierce the apples with the fork.

2. Take a basket and insert a crisper plate in it.

3. Preheat the Ninja Foodi XL Pro Air Oven by adjusting the temperature to 325 degrees F for 3 minutes.

4. Cover the basket with foil over the riper plate.

5. Put the apples on the foil and sprinkle lemon juice and brown sugar on top.

6. Put butter pieces on top as well.

7. Select air fry mode of Ninja Foodi XL Pro Air Oven and press start.

8. After 25 minutes remove the basket and sprinkle granulated sugar on apple pieces.

9. Again, press start and air fry for 20 minutes.

10. Once apples are baked, serve them with listed toppings.

Serving Suggestion: Serve it with ice-cream

Variation Tip: skip the sugar if want low Carb snack

Nutritional Information per Serving: Calories 743 | Fat 36.7g | Sodium 277mg | Carbs 100g | Fiber 3.5g | Sugar 89g | Protein 5.7g

Beef Jerky

Prep Time: 15 Minutes| Cook Time: 7 hours| Makes: 2 Servings

Ingredients:

- 1/3 cup soy sauce
- 1 tablespoon Worcestershire sauce
- 4 tablespoons dark brown sugar
- ½ teaspoon ground black pepper
- ½ teaspoon garlic powder
- ½ teaspoon onion powder
- 1 teaspoon paprika
- 1 teaspoon kosher salt
- 1 pound beef rib eye, uncooked and cut into 1/4-inch slices

Preparation:

1. Combine the entire listed ingredient in a bowl excluding beef.
2. Pour marinade into a plastic zip-lock bag.
3. Add beef to the zip-lock plastic bag and let the beef marinate in it for a few hours.
4. Afterward, take out the beef and drain excess liquid.
5. Remove the crisper plate from the basket of the oven and add meat.
6. Then put it back to the basket.
7. put basket in the oven.
8. Select the "DEHYDRATE" function and set the timer to 7 hours at 250 degrees F.
9. Once done, take out beef jerky and serve.

Serving Suggestion: fried rice

Variation Tip: you can use tamari sauce or coconut amino instead of soy sauce

Nutritional Information per Serving: Calories 572 | Fat 20g |Sodium 3788mg | Carbs 23 g | Fiber 1g | Sugar 20g | Protein 68g

Crispy Potatoes with Mayo

Prep Time: 10 Minutes| Cook Time: 25 Minutes | Makes: 2 Servings

Ingredients:

- 1 pound baby potatoes, cut in slices
- 4 tablespoons olive oil
- 2 teaspoons hot paprika, divided
- 1 tablespoon smoked paprika, divided
- 1 tablespoon garlic powder, divided
- salt, to taste
- 1/2 cup mayonnaise

Preparation:

1. Take a mixing bowl and toss potatoes in it along with olive oil.
2. Add smoked paprika, hot paprika, garlic powder, and salt.
3. Select the air fry and preheat the ninja oven to 360 degrees F for 2 minutes.
4. Then place potatoes on a baking sheet or pan and put it in the oven.
5. Set temperature to 360 degrees F and set time to 25 minutes.
6. Halfway through remove the baking pan from the oven and toss the ingredients.
7. When cooking is complete, serve.

Serving Suggestion: Serve it with mayonnaise

Variation Tip: use any variation of potatoes you liked, it works fine with all the varieties.

Nutritional Information per Serving: Calories 625 | Fat 48g | Sodium 520 mg | Carbs 47g | Fiber 7g | Sugar 6.4g | Protein 7.6g

Brussels Sprouts With Bacon

Prep Time: 10 Minutes| Cook Time: 20 Minutes | Makes: 2 Servings

Ingredients:

- 1 pound of Brussels sprouts
- 6 bacon strips
- 2 tablespoons of garlic powder
- 2 teaspoons of ginger powder
- salt and black pepper, to taste
- 1 tablespoon of olive oil

Preparation:

1. Press air fry and preheat the Ninja Foodi XL Pro Air Oven for 3 minutes at 390 degrees F.

2. Mix all the ingredients in a shallow bowl and then transfer it to the baking tray greased with oil spray.

3. Put the baking tray in the Ninja Foodi XL Pro Air Oven and air fry for 20 minutes.

4. Once half time passed, turn off the Ninja Foodi XL Pro Air Oven and take out the baking dish.

5. Shake the Brussels sprouts and then put it again in the Ninja Foodi XL Pro Air Oven.

6. Air fry until the time completes.

7. Serve.

Serving Suggestion: Serve it with mashed potatoes

Variation Tip: None

Nutritional Information per Serving: Calories 522 | Fat 37.9g | Sodium 809mg | Carbs 31g | Fiber 9.6g | Sugar 7g | Protein 24.3g

Baked Loaded Potatoes

Prep Time: 15 Minutes| Cook Time: 40 Minutes| Makes: 2 Servings

Ingredients:

- 2 large russet potatoes
- ¼ cup of cheddar cheese, shredded
- 8 ounces chili
- Salt, to taste

For Serving

- 2 tablespoons bacon bits
- 4 tablespoons sour cream

Preparation:

1. Pierce the potatoes and place them on a crisper plate, put the plate in the oven basket.

2. Select the bake and let it cook for 35 minutes at 390 degrees F.

3. Afterward, remove the potatoes and slice it.

4. Spoon the middle and add chilies and cheese.

5. Sprinkle salt on top.

6. Return the potatoes to the crisper plate.

7. Select the AIR FRY, set the temperature to 390 degrees F, and set the time to 4 minutes.

8. Once the cooking completes take out the potatoes and serve with the topping of bacon bits and sour cream.

Serving Suggestion: Serve it with cream cheese

Variation Tip: use turkey bacon instead of bacon bits.

Nutritional Information per Serving: Calories 833 | Fat 42g | Sodium 2259mg | Carbs74 g | Fiber 15g | Sugar 4g | Protein 40g

Zucchini Crisps

Prep Time: 10 Minutes| Cook Time: 30 Minutes| Makes: 2 Servings

Ingredients:

- 2 large zucchini, cut in sticks or round
- salt, to taste
- 1 cup all-purpose flour
- 3 eggs, beaten
- 2.5 cups bread crumbs
- 1/3 cup Parmesan cheese, grated
- 1 tablespoon garlic powder
- 1 teaspoon onion powder

Preparation:

1. Put zucchini in a bowl and add salt, let it sit for a while to drain excess liquid.

2. In a medium sized bowl mix the cheese, garlic powder, bread crumbs, onion powder, and salt.

3. Whisk the eggs in a bowl.

4. Place flour in a shallow bowl separately.

5. Toss zucchini in egg wash, then in flour, and at the end in bread crumb mixture.

6. Put it in a crisper plate and add it to the basket.

7. Put the basket in the Ninja Foodi XL Pro Air Oven.

8. Air fry at 360 degrees F for 30 minutes.

9. Halfway through toss the zucchini.

10. Once it's done, serve.

Serving Suggestion: Serve it with marinara sauce

Variation Tip: use Panko bread crumbs

Nutritional Information per Serving: Calories 864 | Fat 24g | Sodium 2277 mg | Carbs 116g | Fiber g | Sugar 7g | Protein 47 g

Blue Cheese Chicken Wings

Prep Time: 10 Minutes| Cook Time: 22 Minutes | Makes: 4 Servings

Ingredients:

- 2 garlic cloves minced
- 1 teaspoon of mustard
- ½ teaspoon of Paprika powder
- Salt and black pepper to taste
- 4 tablespoons of canola oil
- Oil spray, for greasing
- 12 chicken wings
- 1 cup blue cheese, for coating

Preparation:

1. In a shallow bowl mix salt, garlic, black pepper, mustard, paprika, and canola oil.

2. Coat the chicken wings with the rub.

3. Take mesh basket and grease with oil spray.

4. Put the chicken wings into the mesh basket.

5. Preheat the Ninja oven at 357 degrees for 5 minutes.

6. After the preheating is done put the mesh basket in the Ninja Foodi XL Pro Air Oven.

7. Bake it for 22 minutes until crispy and brown from the top.

8. Once the chicken is cooked dredge it in blue cheese for fine coating.

9. Enjoy.

Serving Suggestion: Serve it with your favorite dipping sauce

Variation Tip: Use olive oil instead of canola oil

Nutritional Information per Serving: Calories 1080 | Fat 60g | Sodium 848mg | Carbs 1.1g | Fiber 0.1g | Sugar 0.2g | Protein 134g

Jalapeno Poppers

Prep Time: 15 Minutes| Cook Time: 15 Minutes | Makes: 5 Servings

Ingredients:

- 6 ounces of cream cheese, softened

- 6oucnes of shredded cheddar cheese

- salt, to taste

- 10jalapeño peppers, cut in half, seed removed

- 10 strips of bacon, uncooked

Direction:

1. Preheat the oven by selecting AIR FRY at 360°F, for 3 minutes.

2. Meanwhile, take a mixing bowl and whisk together cheddar, salt, and cream cheese.

3. Fill the jalapeno paper with the cheese mixture.

4. Wrap each pepper with a bacon strip.

5. Place it on a grease baking pan.

6. Put the pan in the oven and set the timer to 15 minutes at 360 degrees F.

7. After 5 minutes, flip the poppers.

8. Once the cooking cycle complete, serve warm.

Serving Suggestion: Serve it with ranch

Variation Tip: you can use parmesan cheese instead of cheddar cheese.

Nutritional Information per Serving: Calories 551 | Fat50 g | Sodium 1523 mg | Carbs 4.1g | Fiber 1.1g | Sugar 1.2g | Protein 20g

French Fries

Prep Time: 10 Minutes| Cook Time: 20 Minutes | Makes: 2 Servings

Ingredients:

* 1 pound of Idaho potatoes, cut into sticks

* salt, to taste

* 1 tablespoon of canola oil

Preparation:

1. Cut the potatoes into 2-inch strips and soak them in cold water for 30 minutes.

2. Drain and pat dry the potatoes.

3. Preheat the Ninja oven at 360 degrees F for 3 minutes.

4. Take a bowl and add potatoes, salt, and canola oil.

5. Toss all the ingredients well.

6. Transfer it to a baking dish and place it inside a ninja oven.

7. Set a timer to 25 minutes at 390 degrees F by selecting Bake.

8. After 15 minutes, turn off the oven and toss the fries.

9. Complete the cooking cycle.

10. Once 25 minutes pass, serve hot.

Serving Suggestion: Serve it with ketchup

Variation Tip: Use olive oil instead of canola oil

Nutritional Information per Serving: Calories 218 | Fat 5g |Sodium 91mg | Carbs 35g | Fiber 5g | Sugar 2g | Protein 2g

Mixed Nuts

Prep Time: 10 Minutes| Cook Time: 15 Minutes | Makes: 4 Servings

Ingredients:

- 1 cup cashew
- 1/2 cup almond
- 1/2 cup peanut or walnuts
- ¼ cup honey
- Pinch of sea salt
- 1/3 teaspoon of paprika
- 1/2 teaspoon of cinnamon
- ½ cup brown sugar

Preparation:

1. In a bowl mix, all the ingredients listed above.

2. Transfer the nuts to the roasting pan.

3. Place pan inside a ninja oven.

4. Select bake and adjust the time to 15 minutes at 360degrees F.

5. Once nuts get roasted, take out and serve.

Serving Suggestion: Serve it with tea or coffee

Variation Tip: use personal preferred nuts.

Nutritional Information per Serving: Calories 503 | Fat 30g | Sodium 73mg | Carbs 52g | Fiber 4g | Sugar 38g | Protein 12g

Chapter 3: Chicken & Poultry Recipes

Chicken Stir Fry

Prep Time: 15 Minutes | Cook Time: 25 Minutes | Makes: 2 Servings

Ingredients:

- 1 pound chicken breasts cut into cubes
- 2 red bell pepper, thinly sliced
- ½ yellow bell pepper, thinly sliced
- 2 orange bell pepper, thinly sliced
- 1 carrot, thinly sliced
- 1/4 cup stir fry sauce
- ¼ cup corn, drained
- ½ cup broccoli, cut in florets
- 2 teaspoons sesame seeds, for garnish
- oil spray, for greasing

Direction:

1. Take a bowl and add chicken, bell peppers, corn, broccoli, and carrots in a bowl.
2. Use an oil spray to coat the ingredient with oil.
3. Put the ingredients in a ninja sheet pan.
4. Turn on the air roast and set the timer to 25 minutes at 400 degrees F.
5. Garnish with sesame seeds and stir fry sauce.

Serving Suggestion: Serve it with your favorite dipping sauce

Variation Tip: Use olive oil instead of oil spray.

Nutritional Information per Serving: Calories 525 | Fat 19g | Sodium 230mg | Carbs 17g | Fiber 3.8g | Sugar 8.5g | Protein 67g

Roasted Chicken with Apple

Prep Time: 20 minutes | Cook Time: 25 minutes | makes: 4 servings

Ingredients:

- 3 gala apples, peeled and sliced
- 6 tablespoons unsalted butter
- 2 tablespoons orange zest
- 1 teaspoon cinnamon
- 1.5 pounds of whole chicken, pieces or cut in half
- Salt and black pepper, pinch
- 2 teaspoons of ginger garlic paste
- Olive oil, for greasing

Preparation:

1. Grease a ninja oven baking pan with olive oil.

2. Cover the bottom of the pan with slices of apple.

3. Take a bowl and combine, cinnamon, butter, zest, ginger garlic paste, salt, and black pepper.

4. Rub the chicken pieces with the mixture.

5. Put the chicken on the top of apple slices in the oven pan.

6. Turn on the Ninja Foodi XL Pro Air Oven and set the timer to 25 minutes at 390 degrees F.

7. Roast the chicken until internal temperature reaches 165 degrees F.

8. Serve the chicken with caramelized apples from the bottom.

9. Enjoys hot.

Serving Suggestion: Serve it with coleslaw

Variation Tip: None

Nutritional Information per Serving: Calories 529 | Fat 37g | Sodium 260mg | Carbs 13.3 g| Fiber 2.1g | Sugar 10g | Protein 30g

Yogurt Chicken

Prep Time: 15 minutes | Cook Time: 35minutes | makes: 2 servings

Ingredients:

- 3-4 chicken breasts
- 1/3 cup yogurt
- 1/2 teaspoon cumin
- 1/4 teaspoon turmeric
- 1/4 teaspoon red chili flakes
- 1/3 teaspoon lemon zest
- 1/4 teaspoon black pepper
- salt, to taste
- oil spray, for greasing

Preparation:

1. Combine yogurt with listed spices and ingredients.

2. Marinate chicken breast in the marinate.

3. Let it sit for 20 minutes.

4. Preheat the Ninja Foodi XL Pro Air Oven by selecting AIR FRY, at 300 degrees F for 3 minutes.

5. After preheating is complete, select air fry mode and adjust the time to 35 minutes at 310 degrees F.

6. Put the chicken breast in oil greased baking sheet pan and place it in ninja oven.

7. Once done, serve.

Serving Suggestion: Serve it with chili sauce

Variation Tip: Use vinegar instead of lemon zest

Nutritional Information per Serving: Calories 451 | Fat 17.6g | Sodium 296mg | Carbs 3.5g | Fiber 0.2g | Sugar 2.9g | Protein 65g

Buffalo wings

Prep Time: 15 Minutes | Cook Time: 25 Minutes | Makes: 2 Servings

Ingredients:

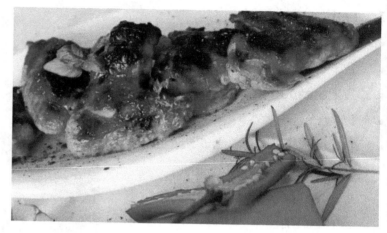

- 8 chicken wings
- 2 tablespoons butter
- 1/4 cup hot sauce
- 1 clove of garlic, minced
- 1/4 teaspoon paprika
- 1/4 teaspoon cayenne pepper
- Salt and black pepper, to taste

Preparation:

1. Take a bowl and combine all the listed ingredients.
2. Marinate the chicken wings in it for 20 minutes.
3. Turn on the air fry mode of Ninja Foodi XL Pro Air Oven and set the temperature to 375 degrees F for 2 minutes.
4. Once preheating done, add chicken wings to the oil greased sheet pan.
5. Turn on air frying mode and set the timer to 20 minutes.
6. After10 minutes of cooking use a tong to flip the chicken wings.
7. Once the cooking cycle completes, serve, and enjoy.

Serving Suggestion: Serve it with your favorite dipping sauce

Variation Tip: Use olive oil instead of butter.

Nutritional Information per Serving: Calories 606 | Fat 27g | Sodium 292mg | Carbs 0g | Fiber 0.3g | Sugar 0.4g | Protein 84g

BBQ Chicken Wings

Prep Time: 15 minutes | Cook Time: 25 minutes | makes: 4 servings

Ingredients:

- 6 tablespoons BBQ sauce
- 2 tablespoon brown sugar
- ½ tablespoon ginger powder
- salt and black pepper, to taste
- ½ teaspoon of paprika
- 1/3 cup honey
- 2.5 pounds chicken wings

Preparation:

1. In a large bowl mix BBQ sauce. Brown sugar, honey, paprika, salt, black pepper, and ginger powder.

2. Marinate chicken wings in it for few hours.

3. Preheat the ninja oven for 3 minutes at 400 degrees.

4. Transfer the wings from the bowl to the baking tray.

5. Air roast the wing in ninja oven for 25 minutes.

6. After10 minutes of cooking use tongs to flip the chicken wings.

7. Once cooking is complete and wings are done, take out the chicken and serve.

Serving Suggestion: Serve it with your favorite dipping sauce

Variation Tip: Use olive oil to mist the wings.

Nutritional Information per Serving: Calories 680 | Fat 21.2g | Sodium 500mg | Carbs 36.6g | Fiber 0.4g | Sugar 33.7g | Protein 82g

Cajun Spice Chicken

Prep Time: 15 Minutes | Cook Time: 20 Minutes | Makes: 2 Servings

Ingredients:

*   1 pound chicken breast, uncooked and skinless

*   2 tablespoons oil, divided

*   2 tablespoons Cajun seasoning

*   3 sweet potatoes, peeled, cut into cubes

*   1 cup broccoli cut in florets

*   Salt and black pepper

Preparation:

1. Take a bowl and add oil and Cajun seasoning.

2. Rub the chicken breast with the rub.

3. Put the chicken in the ninja foodie pan along with broccoli and sweet potatoes.

4. Sprinkle salt and black pepper on top.

5. Turn on the Ninja Foodi XL Pro Air Oven and select air roast.

6. Set a timer to 20 minutes at 400 degrees F.

7. Once preheating done, add the chicken pan to the oven.

8. When the internal temperature of the chicken reaches 165 degrees F, serve it, and enjoy it.

Serving Suggestion: Serve it with your favorite dipping sauce or rice

Variation Tip: None

Nutritional Information per Serving: Calories 562 | Fat 18.4 g | Sodium 388mg | Carbs 42.3g | Fiber 7g | Sugar 9g | Protein 52g

Honey Sriracha Lime Chicken Wings

Prep Time: 15 minutes | Cook Time: 25 minutes | makes: 4 servings

Ingredients:

- 4 tablespoons Sriracha sauce
- 1/3 cup honey
- 4 tablespoons soy sauce
- 2 tablespoons brown sugar
- ½ tablespoon ground ginger
- Zest and juice of 2 limes
- 2.5 pounds chicken wings

Preparation:

1. Take a bowl and combine wings with listed ingredients.

2. refrigerate it for at least 1-hour

3. Turn on the air fry mode of Ninja Foodi XL Pro Air Oven and set the temperature to 400 degrees F for 25 minutes.

4. once preheating done, add chicken to a sheet pan and cook for 25 minutes

5. After 10 minutes of cooking use a tong to flip the chicken wings.

6. cook for additional 15 minutes

7. Once done, take out the chicken and serve.

Serving Suggestion: Serve it with blue cheese or ranch

Variation Tip: Use lemons instead of lime

Nutritional Information per Serving: Calories 652 | Fat 22g | Sodium 1148mg | Carbs 30g | Fiber 0.3g | Sugar 28g | Protein 83g

Spice-Rubbed Chicken Breasts with Chimichurri

Prep Time: 15 minutes | Cook Time: 35 minutes | makes: 2 servings

Ingredients:

- salt and black pepper, to taste
- ½ tablespoon paprika
- 1 tablespoon chili powder
- 2 tablespoons ground fennel
- 2 teaspoons onion powder
- 1 teaspoon garlic powder
- ½ teaspoon ground cumin
- 2 chicken breasts, uncooked
- 2 tablespoons canola oil

CHIMICHURRI Ingredients:

- 1/3 cup olive oil
- 1/3 bunch fresh cilantro
- 1/3 bunch fresh parsley
- 2 shallots, peeled, cut in quarters
- 5 cloves garlic, peeled
- Zest and juice of 1 lemon
- salt, to taste

Preparation:

1. In a large bowl mix all the dry spices including salt, paprika, chili powder, fennel, black pepper, onion powder, garlic powder, and cumin.

2. Rub the chicken breasts with the dry rub.

3. Coat the chicken with canola oil.

4. Put the crisper plate in the oven basket and put it in Ninja Foodi XL Pro Air Oven.

5. Preheat oven by selecting AIR FRY, at 300 degrees F for 3 minutes.

6. Afterward, select air fry mode and adjust time to35 minutes at 300 degrees F.

7. Put the chicken in the basket and cook until the cooking cycle complete.

8. Meanwhile, combine all the Chimichurri ingredients in a ninja blender and pulse into a paste.

9. Afterward, remove chicken from the basket and serve with Chimichurri sauce.

Serving Suggestion: Serve it with ranch dressing

Variation Tip: Use olive oil instead of canola oil

Nutritional Information per Serving: Calories 750 | Fat 60.2g | Sodium 251mg | Carbs 12g | Fiber 4g | Sugar 1.7g | Protein 45g

Teriyaki Glazed Chicken

Prep Time: 15 Minutes | Cook Time: 22 Minutes | Makes: 4 Servings

Ingredients:

- 2 pounds chicken, boneless
- oil spray, for greasing

Teriyaki Glaze Ingredients

- ¼ cup Soy Sauce
- ¼ cup Japanese cooking wine
- ½ cup Brown Sugar
- 2 tablespoons of Lime Juice
- 1/2 cup Orange Juice
- 1 teaspoon of ginger, ground
- ½ teaspoon garlic

Preparation:

1. Mix all the teriyaki glaze ingredients in a shallow bowl and add chicken pieces to it.
2. Let it marinate for a few minutes.
3. Now preheat the ninja oven at 392 degrees F for 5 minutes.
4. Use a baking sheet/ pan and grease it with oil spray.
5. add chicken pieces along with sauce to the pan and put the pan in Ninja Foodi XL Pro Air Oven air fry at 400 for 20 -22 minutes.
6. Once done, serve and enjoy.

Serving Suggestion: Serve it with mashed potatoes

Variation Tip: Use can skip the sugar if do not like the sweet touch.

Nutritional Information per Serving: Calories 437 | Fat 7g | Sodium 1047mg | Carbs 22g | Fiber 0.3g | Sugar 20g | Protein 67g

Tarragon-Mustard Chicken

Prep Time: 20 minutes | Cook Time: 25 minutes | makes: 2 servings

Ingredients:

- 1 pound chicken breast, cubed
- 2 tablespoons of olive oil, melted
- 2 tablespoons Dijon mustard
- 2 teaspoons dried tarragon leaves
- 2 teaspoons sugar
- 1 teaspoon lemon juice
- Salt and pepper, to taste
- oil spray, for greasing

Direction:

1. Take a Ninja Foodi XL Pro Air Oven baking pan and grease it with oil spray.

2. Take a bowl and combine olive oil, Dijon mustard, tarragon leaves, sugar, lemon juice, salt, pepper.

3. Coat the chicken breast with the rub.

4. Turn on the ninja oven and set the timer to 5 minutes at 390 degrees F.

5. Once preheating done, put the chicken in the baking pan /sheet and put it in Ninja Foodi XL Pro Air Oven and air fry for 25 minutes at 390 degrees F.

6. Once done, serve.

Serving Suggestion: Serve it with ketchup

Variation Tip: Use stevia instead of sugar

Nutritional Information per Serving: Calories 500 | Fat 20g | Sodium 250mg | Carbs 5.2g | Fiber0.6g | Sugar 4.2g | Protein 48g

Whole Chicken Roast

Prep Time: 15 Minutes | Cook Time: 25-30 minutes | Makes: 4 Servings

Ingredients:

- 2.5 pounds chicken, whole
- ½ cup canola oil
- 1 teaspoon red pepper flakes
- 2 teaspoons of Brown Sugar
- 2 lemons juice
- 1 teaspoon of cumin
- 1 teaspoon of paprika
- 1teasppoon of lemon zest
- 2 teaspoons thyme, chopped
- 1 teaspoon d rosemary, chopped
- Salt and fresh black pepper, to taste

Preparation:

1. Cut the chicken from the top by placing it on a cutting board.
2. Remove the backbone of the chicken.
3. now in a shallow bowl mix all the listed ingredients along with chicken
4. Rub the chicken with ingredients.
5. Preheat the Ninja Foodi XL Pro Air Oven to 400 degrees F for 5 minutes.
6. Then transfer the chicken to the baking pan cover with aluminum foil.
7. Air roast the chicken in the oven for 25 minutes at 390 degrees F.
8. After25 minutes check and cook for a few minutes more if needed then serve by resting for a while.

Serving Suggestion: Serve it with your favorite dipping sauce

Variation Tip: None

Nutritional Information per Serving: Calories 681 | Fat 36g | Sodium 181mg | Carbs 2.6g | Fiber 0.6g | Sugar 1.6g | Protein 82g

Cheesy Chicken

Prep Time: 15 minutes | Cook Time: 12 minutes | makes: 2 servings

Ingredients:

- 1 pound chicken breasts cut into cubes
- 2 tablespoons olive oil
- Avocado, sliced
- Sour cream, for garnish
- 1 cup cheddar cheese, shaving

Ingredients for Nacho Seasoning

- ½ tablespoon fresh lemon juice
- ½ tablespoon fresh lime juice
- ½ teaspoon ground cumin
- 1/2 cup fresh cilantro, finely chopped
- 2 teaspoons onion powder
- 2 teaspoons chili powder
- Salt, to taste

Preparation:

1. Take a bowl and mix oil and chicken in it.

2. Then add all the nacho seasoning to the bowl.

3. Select the air roast of the Ninja Foodi XL Pro Air Oven and set the temperature to 350 degrees F, for 15 minutes.

4. Once preheating complete add chicken to a pan and put it in the oven.

5. Air roast for 12 minutes at 350 degrees F.

6. Once done, remove it from the oven and serve with sour cream, cheese, and avocado.

Serving Suggestion: Serve it with tortilla chips

Variation Tip: Use personally preferred cheese.

Nutritional Information per Serving: Calories 984 | Fat 69g | Sodium 525mg | Carbs 9 g | Fiber 0.7g | Sugar 0.8g | Protein 81 g

Chicken Tikka Masala

Prep Time: 15 minutes | Cook Time: 25 minutes | makes: 2 servings

Ingredients:

- 1 pound chicken breasts, chopped into bite-size pieces
- 1/3 cup fat-free Greek yogurt
- 1 teaspoon Garam Masala
- 2 tablespoons lemon juice
- Salt and black pepper, to taste
- 1/4 teaspoon ginger, powder
- 2 tablespoons of olive oil

Preparation:

1. In a bowl mix, all the ingredients coat the chicken breasts with the rub.
2. Put the crisper plate in the frying basket and put it in Ninja Foodi XL Pro Air Oven.
3. Preheat oven by selecting AIR FRY, at 300 degrees F for 5 minutes.
4. Select air fry mode and adjust time to25 minutes at 350 degrees F.
5. Put the chicken in a basket and air fry in Ninja Foodi XL Pro Air Oven once done, take out the chicken and serve.

Serving Suggestion: Serve it with your favorite dipping sauce

Variation Tip: Use canola oil instead of olive oil

Nutritional Information per Serving: Calories 655 | Fat 30g | Sodium 265mg | Carbs 7.5g | Fiber 7g | Sugar 7.3g | Protein 84g

Turkey in Ninja Oven

Prep Time: 15 minutes | Cook Time: 25 minutes | makes: 2 servings

Ingredients:

- 1 pound turkey breast, rib removed
- 2 tablespoon olive oil
- salt, to taste
- 2 tablespoons dry turkey seasoning

Preparation:

1. Rub the turkey breast with olive oil, salt, and dry turkey seasoning.
2. Preheat the Ninja Foodi XL Pro Air Oven at 350 degrees F for 3 minutes.
3. Put the crisper plate in the oven basket and put it in the unit.
4. Preheat oven by selecting AIR FRY, at 300 degrees F for 3 minutes.
5. Then select air fry mode and adjust the time to 35 minutes at 310 degrees F.
6. Put the turkey breasts in the basket and cook until the cycle complete.
7. Let it rest for10 minutes, before serving.

Serving Suggestion: Serve it with your favorite dipping sauce or mashed potatoes

Variation Tip: None

Nutritional Information per Serving: Calories 356 | Fat 17.8g | Sodium 2380mg | Carbs 9.6g | Fiber 1.1g | Sugar 8g | Protein 38.7g

Country Style Chicken Wings

Prep Time: 20 Minutes | Cook Time: 25 Minutes | Makes: 4 Servings

Ingredients:

- 2 pounds of chicken wings
- 10 ounces of Plum sauce
- 1/3 cup brown sugar
- 6 tablespoons soy sauce
- 2 tablespoons cornstarch
- 1/3 cup orange juice
- Salt and pepper, to taste

Preparation:

1. Take a bowl and combine all the listed ingredients.

2. Marinate it for 20 minutes.

3. Turn on the air fry mode and set the temperature to 375 degrees F for 2 minutes.

4. Once preheating done, add chicken wings to a sheet pan.

5. Turn on the air frying mode of Ninja Foodi XL Pro Air Oven and set the timer to 20 minutes.

6. After10 minutes of cooking use a tong to flip the chicken wings.

7. Once the cooking cycle completes, serve, and enjoy.

Serving Suggestion: Serve it with your favorite dipping sauce

Variation Tip: Use lemon juice instead of orange juice.

Nutritional Information per Serving: Calories 522 | Fat 18g | Sodium 1552mg | Carbs 21g | Fiber 0.5g | Sugar 15g | Protein 68g

Chicken Meat Patties

Prep Time: 15 Minutes | Cook Time: 20 Minutes | Makes: 3 Servings

Ingredients:

- 1.5 pounds of chicken meat, ground
- 1 tablespoon of olive oil
- ½ cup shallots, chopped
- 2 green peppers, chopped
- 1 teaspoon coriander powder
- ½ teaspoon of turmeric
- ¼ teaspoon of cumin, ground
- 1 egg, whisked
- salt, to taste

Preparation:

1. Take a shallow bowl and mix all the ingredients.

2. Make meat patties of the mixture and place it on a baking sheet that is greased with oil spray.

3. Bake it in Ninja Foodi XL Pro Air Oven for20 minutes at 400 degrees F.

4. Once done, serve.

Serving Suggestion: Serve it with your favorite dipping sauce

Variation Tip: Use olive oil instead of canola oil

Nutritional Information per Serving: Calories 529 | Fat 23g | Sodium 272 mg | Carbs 5.6g | Fiber 1.5g | Sugar 2g | Protein 68g

Chapter 4: Fish & Seafood Recipes

Lobster Tail Casserole

Prep Time: 15 minutes | Cook Time: 16 minutes | makes: 6 servings

Ingredients:

- 2 tablespoons fresh tarragon, chopped
- 1 lb. salmon fillets, cut into 8 equal pieces
- 16 large sea scallops
- 16 large prawns, peeled and deveined
- 1/2 teaspoon paprika
- 8 lobster tails, meat only, cubed
- 1/3 cup butter
- 1/4 cup white wine
- 1/4 cup lemon juice
- 2 medium garlic cloves, minced
- 1/4 teaspoon ground cayenne pepper

Preparation:

1. Whisk butter with lemon juice, wine, garlic, tarragon, paprika, salt, and cayenne pepper in a small saucepan.
2. Stir cook this mixture over medium heat for 1 minute.
3. Toss the seafood in the Ninja baking dish and pour the butter mixture on top.
4. Transfer this baking dish to the Ninja XL Pro Air Fry Oven and Close its door.
5. Select the "bake" mode using the Function Keys and select Rack Level 2.
6. Set its cooking time to 15 minutes and temperature to 450 degrees F then press "START/STOP" to initiate preheating.
7. Serve warm.

Serving Suggestion: Serve the casserole with toasted bread slices.

Variation Tip: Add crab roe and peas to the casserole.

Nutritional Information Per Serving:

Calories 248 | Fat 16g |Sodium 94mg | Carbs 31.4g | Fiber 0.4g | Sugar 3g | Protein 24.9g

Haddock Cream Casserole

Prep Time: 15 minutes | Cook Time: 20 minutes | makes: 8 servings

Ingredients:

- 8 oz haddock, skinned and diced
- 1 lb scallops
- 1 lb large shrimp, peeled and deveined
- 3 garlic cloves, minced
- 1/2 cup heavy cream
- 1/2 cup Swiss cheese, shredded
- 2 tablespoons Parmesan, grated
- Paprika, to taste
- Sea salt and black pepper, to taste

Preparation:

1. Toss shrimp, scallops, and haddock chunks in the Ninja baking dish greased with cooking spray.
2. Drizzle salt, black pepper, and minced garlic over the seafood mix.
3. Top this seafood with cream, Swiss cheese, paprika, and Parmesan cheese.
4. Transfer the dish to the Ninja XL Pro Air Fry Oven and Close its door.
5. Select the "Bake" Mode using the Function Keys and select Rack Level 2.
6. Set its cooking time to 20 minutes and temperature to 375 degrees F then press "START/STOP" to initiate preheating.
7. Serve warm.

Serving Suggestion: Serve the casserole with toasted bread slices.

Variation Tip: Drizzle breadcrumbs on top for a crispy touch.

Nutritional Information Per Serving:

Calories 457 | Fat 19g |Sodium 557mg | Carbs 19g | Fiber 1.8g | Sugar 1.2g | Protein 32.5g

White Fish with Lemon Pepper

Prep Time: 15 minutes | Cook Time: 12 minutes | makes: 2 servings

Ingredients:

- 2 (6 ounces) tilapia filets
- 1/2 teaspoon garlic powder
- 1/2 teaspoon lemon pepper seasoning
- 1/2 teaspoon onion powder
- Salt, to taste
- Black pepper, to taste
- Fresh chopped parsley
- Lemon wedges

Preparation:

1. Rub the tilapia fillets with olive oil, garlic powder, onion powder, lemon pepper, salt, and black pepper liberally.
2. Place the seasoned fish fillets on the Air Fryer.
3. Transfer this Air Fryer basket to the Ninja XL Pro Air Fry Oven and Close its door.
4. Select the "Air Fry" Mode using the Function Keys and select Rack Level 2.
5. Set its cooking time to 12 minutes and temperature to 360 degrees F then press "START/STOP" to initiate preheating.
6. Garnish with parsley and lemon wedges.
7. Serve warm.

Serving Suggestion: Serve the fish with mashed potatoes.

Variation Tip: Add dried herbs to the coating.

Nutritional Information Per Serving:

Calories 378 | Fat 7g |Sodium 316mg | Carbs 16.2g | Fiber 0.3g | Sugar 0.3g | Protein 26g

Garlic Parmesan Shrimp

Prep Time: 15 minutes | Cook Time: 10 minutes | makes: 4 servings

Ingredients:

- 1 lb. shrimp, deveined and peeled
- 1 tablespoon olive oil
- 1 teaspoon salt
- 1 teaspoon fresh cracked pepper
- 1 tablespoon lemon juice
- 6 garlic cloves, diced
- ½ cup parmesan cheese, grated

Preparation:

1. Toss the shrimp with olive oil, lemon juice, salt, garlic, and black pepper in a large bowl.
2. Cover the shrimp and refrigerate for 3 hours.
3. Add parmesan cheese to the shrimp and toss it gently to coat.
4. Spread the shrimp over the Air Fryer basket and transfer to the Ninja XL Pro Air Fry Oven, then close its door.
5. Select the "bake" mode using the Function Keys and select Rack Level 2.
6. Set its cooking time to 10 minutes and temperature to 350 degrees F then press "START/STOP" to initiate preheating.
7. Serve warm.

Serving Suggestion: Serve the shrimp with crusted fish and boiled eggs.

Variation Tip: Drizzle cheddar cheese on top for a rich taste.

Nutritional Information Per Serving:

Calories 351 | Fat 4g |Sodium 236mg | Carbs 19.1g | Fiber 0.3g | Sugar 0.1g | Protein 36g

Baked Shrimp with Garlic Sauce

Prep Time: 15 minutes | Cook Time: 9 minutes | makes: 4 servings

Ingredients:

- 1/4 cup butter
- 1 tablespoon garlic, minced
- 2 tablespoons fresh lemon juice
- Salt and black pepper, to taste
- 1/8 teaspoons red pepper flakes
- 1 ¼ lbs large shrimp, peeled and deveined
- 2 tablespoons fresh parsley, minced

Preparation:

1. Spread the shrimp in the Ninja foodi baking dish.
2. Melt butter in a pan and sauté garlic in it for 30 seconds.
3. Stir in lemon, then pour this mixture over the shrimp.
4. Drizzle salt, black pepper, and red pepper flakes over the shrimp.
5. Gently toss the shrimp, then transfer this dish to Ninja XL Pro Air Fry Oven and Close its door.
6. Select the "Bake" Mode using the Function Keys and select Rack Level 2.
7. Set its cooking time to 9 minutes and temperature to 300 degrees F then press "START/STOP" to initiate preheating.
8. Serve warm.

Serving Suggestion: Serve the shrimp on top of the risotto.

Variation Tip: Add paprika for more spice.

Nutritional Information Per Serving:

Calories 248 | Fat 13g |Sodium 353mg | Carbs 1g | Fiber 0.4g | Sugar 1g | Protein 29g

Dill Seafood Paella

Prep Time: 15 minutes | Cook Time: 30 minutes | makes: 8 servings

Ingredients:

- 1 cup unsalted butter melted
- 3 tablespoons fresh dill, chopped
- 2 tablespoons garlic minced
- Salt, to taste
- Black pepper, to taste
- 24 ounces baby red potato
- 4 fillets cod,
- 30 shrimp raw, peeled, and deveined
- 8 lemon slices
- 4 corn ears, husked and halved

Preparation:

1. Cut the foil sheet into 8- 2 feet squares and place 4 pieces over a working surface.
2. Place the remaining pieces over these pieces to double them.
3. Spray each group of foil sheets with cooking oil to grease them.
4. Now melt butter in a glass bowl and add baby dill, black pepper, salt, and garlic.
5. Mix well and keep this dill butter aside.
6. Place each fish fillet over one square of greased foil, then top it with 6 shrimp, 2 corn halves, ½ cup potatoes, and ¼ of the dill butter.
7. Finally, set 2 lemon slices on top of each fillet and wrap each foil sheet around the toppings.
8. Place the fish pockets inside the Ninja XL Pro Air Fry Oven ad Close its door.
9. Select the "bake" mode using the Function Keys and select Rack Level 2.
10. Set its cooking time to 30 minutes and temperature to 350 degrees F then press "START/STOP" to initiate preheating.
11. Unwrap the baked fish and serve warm with the veggies.
12. Enjoy.

Serving Suggestion: Serve the seafood mix with fried rice.

Variation Tip: Add boiled rice or noodles to the mixture.

Nutritional Information Per Serving:

Calories 321 | Fat 7.4g |Sodium 356mg | Carbs 22.3g | Fiber 2.4g | Sugar 5g | Protein 37.2g

Seafood Mushrooms Casserole

Prep Time: 15 minutes | Cook Time: 25 minutes | makes: 8 servings

Ingredients:

- 5 tablespoons butter
- 4 ounces mushrooms, sliced
- 16 ounces shrimp
- 8 ounces of lobster meat, diced
- 4 ounces crabmeat, diced
- 1/4 cup flour
- 2 cups of milk
- Salt, to taste
- Black pepper, to taste
- 1/4 teaspoon paprika
- 2 teaspoons chives, snipped
- 2 teaspoons parsley, chopped
- 2 tablespoons dry white wine
- 4 tablespoons Parmesan cheese

Preparation:

1. Sauté mushroom with 1 tablespoon butter in a pan until soft.
2. Grease a casserole dish with butter, then add seafood and mushrooms.
3. Melt rest of the butter in a suitable saucepan, then add flour.
4. Stir and cook for 2 minutes, then pour in milk with continuous stirring.
5. Cook until it bubbles, then add wine, herbs, and seasonings.
6. Pour this sauce over the seafood and top it with cheese.
7. Transfer the seafood casserole to the Air Fry Oven.
8. Select the "bake" mode using the Function Keys and select Rack Level 2.
9. Set its cooking time to 20 minutes and temperature to 350 degrees F then press "START/STOP" to initiate preheating.
10. Serve immediately.

Serving Suggestion: Serve the casserole with toasted bread slices.

Variation Tip: Add chopped veggies and mushrooms.

Nutritional Information Per Serving:

Calories 415 | Fat 15g |Sodium 634mg | Carbs 14.3g | Fiber 1.4g | Sugar 1g | Protein 23.3g

Halibut Scallops Bake

Prep Time: 15 minutes | Cook Time: 12 minutes | makes: 8 servings

Ingredients:

- 2 (4 ounces) halibut fillets, cubed
- 6 scallops
- 6 shrimp, peeled and deveined
- 1/3 cup dry white wine
- 2 tablespoons melted butter
- 1 tablespoon lemon juice
- 1/2 teaspoon Old Bay seasoning
- 1 teaspoon garlic, minced
- Salt and pepper to taste
- 1 tablespoon fresh parsley, chopped

Preparation:

1. Toss halibut chunks, shrimp, and scallops in the Ninja baking dish.
2. Whisk wine, lemon juice, and butter in a small bowl and pour over the seafood.
3. Drizzle seasoning, garlic, salt, and black pepper over the seafood mixture.
4. Transfer the baking dish to the Ninja XL Pro Air Fry Oven and Close its door.
5. Select the "bake" mode using the Function Keys and select Rack Level 2.
6. Set its cooking time to 12 minutes and temperature to 450 degrees F then press "START/STOP" to initiate preheating.
7. Garnish with parsley.
8. Serve warm.

Serving Suggestion: Serve the baked seafood with alfredo sauce on top.

Variation Tip: Marinate the seasoned seafood for 20 minutes.

Nutritional Information Per Serving:
Calories 392 | Fat 16g |Sodium 466mg | Carbs 3.9g | Fiber 0.9g | Sugar 0.6g | Protein 48g

Breaded Shrimp

Prep Time: 15 minutes | Cook Time: 4 minutes | makes: 4 servings

Ingredients:

- 1 lb. raw shrimp peeled and deveined
- 1 egg white
- 1/2 cup all-purpose flour
- 3/4 cup panko bread crumbs
- 1 teaspoon paprika
- Montreal Chicken Seasoning to taste
- Salt and pepper to taste
- Cooking spray

Bang Bang Sauce

- 1/3 cup plain Greek yogurt
- 2 tablespoons Sriracha
- 1/4 cup sweet chili sauce

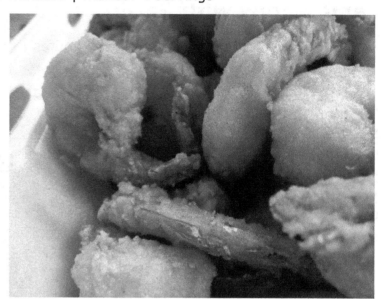

Preparation:

1. Spread flour in one bowl, beat the egg in another, and breadcrumbs in a shallow tray.
2. Season the shrimp with paprika, Montreal seasoning, salt, and black pepper.
3. First coat the shrimp with flour, then dip in the egg and coat with breadcrumbs.
4. Place the shrimps in the Air Fryer basket and spray them with cooking oil.
5. Transfer the Air Fryer basket to the Ninja XL Pro Air Fry Oven and close its door.
6. Select the "bake" mode using the Function Keys and select Rack Level 2.
7. Set its cooking time to 4 minutes and temperature to 400 degrees F then press "START/STOP" to initiate preheating.
8. Meanwhile, mix the yogurt, sriracha, and sweet chili sauce in a bowl.
9. Serve the air fried shrimp with bang bang sauce.
10. Enjoy.

Serving Suggestion: Serve the shrimp with ketchup.

Variation Tip: Use white pepper for a change of flavor.

Nutritional Information Per Serving:

Calories 378 | Fat 21g |Sodium 146mg | Carbs 7.1g | Fiber 0.1g | Sugar 0.4g | Protein 23g

Chapter 5: Beef, Pork, and Lamb

Lamb Chops with Garlic Sauce

Prep Time: 15 minutes | Cook Time: 15 minutes | makes: 8 servings

Ingredients:

- 1 garlic bulb, peeled
- 3 tablespoons olive oil
- Sea salt, to taste
- Black pepper, to taste
- 1 tablespoon fresh oregano, chopped
- 8 lamb chops

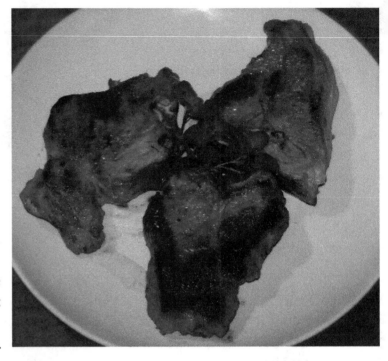

Preparation:

1. Rub lamb chops with oil, oregano, salt, and black pepper.
2. Place 4 of these chops in the casserole dish, then spread the garlic cloves around them.
3. Transfer the chops to the Ninja XL Pro Air Fry Oven and Close its door.
4. Select the "Air Fry" Mode using the Function Keys and select Rack Level 2.
5. Set its cooking time to 10 minutes and temperature to 370 degrees F then press "START/STOP" to initiate preheating.
6. Flip the chops and continue Air frying for another 5 minutes.
7. Cook the remaining four chops following the same steps.
8. Squeeze the baked garlic and mix it with the lamb chops drippings.
9. Serve the chops with garlic mixture on top.
10. Enjoy.

Serving Suggestion: Serve the chops with fresh herbs on top.

Variation Tip: Add butter to the chops before cooking.

Nutritional Information Per Serving:
Calories 405 | Fat 22.7g |Sodium 227mg | Carbs 26.1g | Fiber 1.4g | Sugar 0.9g | Protein 45.2g

Beef Potato Medley

Prep Time: 15 minutes | Cook Time: 1 hr. 30 minutes | makes: 6 servings

Ingredients:

- 3 tablespoons soy sauce
- 1 tablespoon Worcestershire sauce
- 1/4 cup flour
- Salt, to taste
- Black pepper, to taste
- 3 bay leaves
- 3 sprigs thyme
- 2 lbs. lean beef, cubed
- 3 garlic cloves, minced
- 1 carrot, sliced
- 1 onion, sliced
- 6 new potatoes, halved
- 2 celery ribs, sliced
- 1 cup red wine
- 1 cup beef stock
- 2 tablespoons parsley, chopped

Preparation:

1. Whisk soy sauce, seasoning, flour, Worcestershire, thyme, and bay leaves in a casserole dish.
2. Toss in veggies and meat to this mixture and mix well.
3. Finally, pour in red wine and beef stock, then give it a gentle stir.
4. Cover this casserole dish with a foil sheet and poke two-three holes in it.
5. Transfer this casserole dish to the Ninja XL Pro Air Fry Oven and Close its door.
6. Select the "Bake" Mode using the Function Keys and select Rack Level 2.
7. Set its cooking time to 1 hr. 30 minutes and temperature to 350 degrees F then press "START/STOP" to initiate preheating.
8. Serve warm.

Serving Suggestion: Serve the medley with tortilla slices.

Variation Tip: Ground beef can also be used instead.

Nutritional Information Per Serving:
Calories 537 | Fat 20g |Sodium 719mg | Carbs 25.1g | Fiber 0.9g | Sugar 1.4g | Protein 37.8g

Pork Chops with Broccoli

Prep Time: 15 minutes | Cook Time: 10 minutes | makes: 2 servings

Ingredients:

- 2 (5 ounces) bone-in pork chops
- 2 tablespoons avocado oil
- 1/2 teaspoon paprika
- 1/2 teaspoon onion powder
- 1/2 teaspoon garlic powder
- 1 teaspoon salt, divided
- 2 cups broccoli florets
- 2 garlic cloves, minced

Preparation:

1. Rub the chops with half of the oil, salt, garlic powder, onion powder, and paprika liberally.
2. Place these chops in the Air frying sheet of the Ninja XL Pro Air Fry Oven.
3. Toss the broccoli and garlic with remaining oil and salt, then spread them around the pork chops.
4. Transfer the chops and veggies to the Ninja XL Pro Air Fry Oven and Close its door.
5. Select the "Bake" Mode using the Function Keys and select Rack Level 2.
6. Set its cooking time to 5 minutes and temperature to 370 degrees F then press "START/STOP" to initiate preheating.
7. Flip the chops and all the veggies, then continue cooking for another 5 minutes.
8. Serve warm.

Serving Suggestion: Serve the chops with butter cube on top.

Variation Tip: Drizzle parmesan cheese on top before cooking.

Nutritional Information Per Serving:
Calories 395 | Fat 9.5g |Sodium 655mg | Carbs 13.4g | Fiber 0.4g | Sugar 0.4g | Protein 28.3g

Russian Beef

Prep Time: 15 minutes | Cook Time: 60 minutes | makes: 4 servings

Ingredients:

- 1 (2 lbs.) beef tenderloin, sliced
- Salt and black pepper to taste
- 2 onions, sliced
- 1 1/2 cups Cheddar cheese, grated
- 1 cup milk
- 3 tablespoons mayonnaise

Preparation:

1. Slice the beef and season it with salt and black pepper.
2. Place these beef strips in the casserole dish, then add onions, cheddar cheese, milk, and mayonnaise to the beef.
3. Toss well, then transfer this casserole dish to the Ninja XL Pro Air Fry Oven and Close its door.
4. Select the "Bake" Mode using the Function Keys and select Rack Level 2.
5. Set its cooking time to 60 minutes and temperature to 350 degrees F then press "START/STOP" to initiate preheating.
6. Serve warm.

Serving Suggestion: Serve the beef with toasted bread slices.

Variation Tip: Ground chicken or beef can also be used instead of tenderloin.

Nutritional Information Per Serving:

Calories 309 | Fat 25g |Sodium 463mg | Carbs 9.9g | Fiber 0.3g | Sugar 0.3g | Protein 18g

Breaded Pork Chops

Prep Time: 15 minutes | Cook Time: 12 minutes | makes: 3 servings

Ingredients:

- 3 (6ounces) pork chops, rinsed
- Salt, to taste
- Black pepper, to taste
- Garlic powder, to taste
- Smoked paprika, to taste
- 1/2 cup breadcrumbs
- 1 large egg

Preparation:

1. First, rub the pork chops with garlic powder, black pepper, salt, and smoked paprika.
2. Spread the breadcrumbs in a shallow bowl and beat the egg in another bowl.
3. Dip each chop in egg first, then coat it well with breadcrumbs.
4. Place these chops in the Air Fryer basket.
5. Transfer these chops to the Ninja XL Pro Air Fry Oven and Close its door.
6. Select the "Air Fry" Mode using the Function Keys and select Rack Level 2.
7. Set its cooking time to 12 minutes and temperature to 380 degrees F then press "START/STOP" to initiate preheating.
8. Flip the chops after 6 minutes and resume cooking.
9. Serve warm.

Serving Suggestion: Serve the chops with fresh greens.

Variation Tip: Use crushed cornflakes for a more crispy texture.

Nutritional Information Per Serving:
Calories 545 | Fat 36g |Sodium 272mg | Carbs 41g | Fiber 0.2g | Sugar 0.1g | Protein 42.5g

Roast Lamb with Potatoes

Prep Time: 15 minutes | Cook Time: 60 minutes | makes: 6 servings

Ingredients:

- 4 garlic cloves, minced
- 3 tablespoons olive oil
- 1 (2-lb.) boneless lamb shoulder roast
- Salt, to taste
- 1 tablespoon rosemary, chopped
- 2 teaspoons fresh thyme leaves
- Black pepper, to taste
- 2 lb. baby potatoes, halved

Preparation:

1. Whisk garlic, thyme, rosemary, salt, black pepper, and 1 tablespoon oil in a small bowl.
2. Rub this mixture well over the lamb, then place it in a casserole dish.
3. Cover the lamb with potato, then place the dish in the Ninja XL Pro Air Fry Oven and Close its door.
4. Select the "Bake" Mode using the Function Keys and select Rack Level 2.
5. Set its cooking time to 60 minutes and temperature to 370 degrees F then press "START/STOP" to initiate preheating.
6. Slice the roast and serve warm.

Serving Suggestion: Serve the lamb with blue cheese on top.

Variation Tip: Use barbecue sauce for seasoning.

Nutritional Information Per Serving:

Calories 361 | Fat 16g |Sodium 515mg | Carbs 19.3g | Fiber 0.1g | Sugar 18.2g | Protein 33.3g

Spiced Pork Chops

Prep Time: 15 minutes | Cook Time: 18 minutes | makes: 4 servings

Ingredients:

- 1 tablespoon paprika
- 2 teaspoons onion powder
- 2 teaspoons garlic powder
- 1 teaspoon oregano
- Salt, to taste
- Black pepper, to taste
- 2 tablespoons olive oil
- 4 boneless pork chops

Preparation:

1. Season the pork with olive oil, salt, oregano, pepper, paprika, garlic powder, and onion powder.

2. Transfer these chops to the cooking pan of the Ninja XL Pro Air Fry Oven and place it in the Ninja XL Pro Air Fry Oven, then close its door.

3. Select the "bake" mode using the Function Keys and select Rack Level 2.

4. Set its cooking time to 18 minutes and temperature to 400 degrees F then press "START/STOP" to initiate preheating.

5. Serve warm.

Serving Suggestion: Serve the chops with roasted veggies.

Variation Tip: Brush with barbecue sauce instead.

Nutritional Information Per Serving:

Calories 548 | Fat 23g |Sodium 350mg | Carbs 18g | Fiber 6.3g | Sugar 1g | Protein 40.3g

Lamb Leg with Mint Sauce

Prep Time: 15 minutes | Cook Time: 1 hr. 30 minutes | makes: 8 servings

Ingredients:

- 4 lbs. leg of lamb
- 1 bulb of garlic, peeled
- ½ a bunch of fresh rosemary
- 1 lemon, juiced
- 1 teaspoon olive oil

Mint Sauce

- 1 bunch of fresh mint
- 1 teaspoon sugar
- 3 tablespoons wine vinegar

Preparation:

1. Rub the lamb with salt and black pepper, then place it in a casserole dish.
2. Toss the remaining ingredients together in a bowl, then spread it around the lamb.
3. Place the lamb dish in the Ninja XL Pro Air Fry Oven and Close its door.
4. Select the "Bake" Mode using the Function Keys and select Rack Level 2.
5. Set its cooking time to 1 hr. 30 minutes and temperature to 400 degrees F then press "START/STOP" to initiate preheating.
6. Meanwhile, prepare the mint sauce by blending all its ingredients in a blender.
7. Serve the lamb with mint sauce on top.
8. Enjoy.

Serving Suggestion: Serve the lamb leg with roasted bell peppers and cherry tomatoes.

Variation Tip: Wrap the lamb leg with a vegetable of your choice in a foil sheet before baking.

Nutritional Information Per Serving:

Calories 380 | Fat 20g |Sodium 686mg | Carbs 33g | Fiber 1g | Sugar 1.2g | Protein 21g

Garlicky Pork Chops

Prep Time: 15 minutes | Cook Time: 35 minutes | makes: 4 servings

Ingredients:

- 2 lbs. Yukon gold potatoes, diced
- 3 tablespoons canola oil
- 4 bone-in pork loin chops
- 2 tablespoons garlic minced
- 1/2 cup brown sugar packed
- Salt, to taste
- Ground black pepper, to taste

Preparation:

1. Season the potatoes with oil, salt, black pepper, and spread them in the Air Fry sheet.

2. Now whisk brown sugar with salt and black pepper, then season the pork chops with this sweet mixture.

3. Place these chops in the Air Fryer Basket and transfer to the Ninja XL Pro Air Fry Oven. Close its door.

4. Select the "Bake" Mode using the Function Keys and select Rack Level 2.

5. Set its cooking time to 35 minutes and temperature to 375 degrees F then press "START/STOP" to initiate preheating.

6. Serve warm.

Serving Suggestion: Serve the chops with toasted bread slices.

Variation Tip: Add sweet potatoes or squash instead of potatoes.

Nutritional Information Per Serving:

Calories 301 | Fat 5g |Sodium 340mg | Carbs 24.7g | Fiber 1.2g | Sugar 1.3g | Protein 15.3g

Chapter 6: Interesting Recipes

Blooming Onion

Prep Time: 15 minutes | Cook Time: 25 minutes | makes: 2 servings

Ingredients:

Onion

- 1 large yellow onion
- 3 large eggs
- 1 cup breadcrumbs
- 2 teaspoons paprika
- 1 teaspoon garlic powder
- 1 teaspoon onion powder
- 1 teaspoon kosher salt
- 3 tablespoons olive oil

Sauce

- 2/3 cup mayonnaise
- 2 tablespoons. ketchup
- 1 teaspoon horseradish
- 1/2 teaspoon paprika
- 1/2 teaspoon garlic powder

- 1/4 teaspoon dried oregano
- Kosher salt, to taste

Preparation:

1. Slice the onion from top to bottom vertically into 16 sections while keeping the bottom intact.

2. Whisk eggs with 1 tablespoon water in one bowl and mix breadcrumbs with spices in another bowl.

3. Dip the onion in the egg wash and coat with the breadcrumbs.

4. Place the onion in the air fryer basket and spray with cooking oil on top.

5. Set the air fryer basket in the Ninja XL Pro Air Fry Oven.

6. Select the "Air Fry" Mode using the Function Keys and select Rack Level 2.

7. Set its cooking time to 25 minutes and temperature to 375 degrees F then press "START/STOP" to initiate preheating.

8. Mix mayonnaise, horseradish, ketchup, garlic powder, dried oregano, salt, and paprika in a bowl.

9. Serve the onion with the sauce.

10. Enjoy.

Serving Suggestion: Serve the onion with ketchup or hot sauce.

Variation Tip: Use crushed cornflakes for a more crispy texture.

Nutritional Information Per Serving:

Calories 305 | Fat 25g |Sodium 532mg | Carbs 2.3g | Fiber 0.4g | Sugar 2g | Protein 18.3g

Chicken Enchiladas

Prep Time: 15 minutes | Cook Time: 6 minutes | makes: 12 servings

Ingredients:

- 12 corn tortillas
- 1½ cups Mexican Chicken, Shredded
- 2 cups Enchilada Sauce
- 1½ cups Mexican Cheese, Shredded

Preparation:

1. Place six corn tortillas in the air fryer basket at a time.
2. Spray cooking oil on top and set the basket in the Ninja XL Pro Air Fry Oven.
3. Select the "Air Fry" Mode using the Function Keys and select Rack Level 2.
4. Set its cooking time to 3 minutes and temperature to 3425 degrees F then press "START/STOP" to initiate preheating.
5. Divide the shredded chicken and enchiladas sauce in each tortilla.
6. Set the prepared tortillas in a baking tray and drizzle shredded cheese on top.
7. Slide this tray into the Air Fry Oven and close its door.
8. Select the "Broil" Mode using the Function Keys and select Rack Level 2.
9. Set its cooking time to 3 minutes and temperature to 325 degrees F then press "START/STOP" to initiate preheating.
10. Serve warm.

Serving Suggestion: Serve the casserole with toasted bread slices.

Variation Tip: Add cream cheese and pepperoni slices.

Nutritional Information Per Serving:

Calories 305 | Fat 25g |Sodium 532mg | Carbs 2.3g | Fiber 0.4g | Sugar 2g | Protein 18.3g

Baked Potatoes

Prep Time: 15 minutes | Cook Time: 45 minutes | makes: 6 servings

Ingredients:

- 6 large russet potatoes, scrubbed
- 1 tablespoon olive oil
- Kosher salt, to taste
- 1/2 cup butter, softened
- 1/2 cup milk
- 1/2 cup sour cream
- 1 1/2 cup Cheddar cheese, shredded
- 2 green onions, thinly sliced
- Black pepper, to taste

Preparation:

1. Score the potatoes with a fork and rub with salt and oil.
2. Place the potatoes in a baking tray and transfer to the Air Fry Oven.
3. Select the "bake" mode using the Function Keys and select Rack Level 2.
4. Set its cooking time to 40 minutes and temperature to 400 degrees F then press "START/STOP" to initiate preheating.
5. Cut the potatoes from the top lengthwise to make a slit and scoop out some flesh from the center.
6. Add potato flesh, sour cream, milk, and butter to a bowl, then mix well.
7. Stir in green onions, black pepper, salt, and 1 cup cheese, then mix well.
8. Divide and stuff this mixture in the potato slits.
9. Set them in the air fryer basket and place them in the Ninja XL Pro Air Fry Oven.
10. Select the "bake" mode using the Function Keys and select Rack Level 2.
11. Set its cooking time to 5 minutes and temperature to 400 degrees F then press "START/STOP" to initiate preheating.
12. Garnish with green onions.
13. Serve warm.

Serving Suggestion: Serve the potatoes with roasted green beans and cream dip.

Variation Tip: Add crumbled bacon or cooked ground meat to the filling.

Nutritional Information Per Serving:

Calories 305 | Fat 25g |Sodium 532mg | Carbs 2.3g | Fiber 0.4g | Sugar 2g | Protein 18.3g

Whole Turkey with Gravy

Prep Time: 15 minutes | Cook Time: 2 hr. 30 minutes | makes: 20 servings

Ingredients:

- 14 lb. raw Whole Turkey
- 6 tablespoons butter, cut into slices
- 4 garlic cloves, sliced thin
- 1 tablespoon kosher salt, or to taste
- Black pepper, to taste
- Oil to coat turkey
- 1 ½ cups chicken broth
- 3/4 cup flour

Preparation:

1. Mix butter with garlic and stuff it under the turkey skin.
2. Rub salt, black pepper, and oil over turkey.
3. Place the seasoned turkey in the baking tray and pour ½ cup broth on top.
4. Set the tray in the Ninja XL Pro Air Fry Oven and close its door.
5. Select the "Whole Roast" mode using the Function Keys and select Rack Level 2.
6. Set its cooking time to 2 hrs. 30 minutes and temperature to 350 degrees F then press "START/STOP" to initiate preheating.
7. And baste the turkey after every 30 minutes.
8. Then transfer the roasted turkey to a serving plate and cover it with a foil sheet.
9. Pour the turkey cooking juices into a saucepan, add remaining broth and other ingredients.
10. Set the pan over medium heat and cook until it thickens.
11. Pour this sauce over the roasted turkey.
12. Serve warm.

Serving Suggestion: Serve the turkey with fresh lemon juice and herbs on top.

Variation Tip: Stuff the turkey with oranges, lemon, garlic, and onion.

Nutritional Information Per Serving:
Calories 305 | Fat 25g |Sodium 532mg | Carbs 2.3g | Fiber 0.4g | Sugar 2g | Protein 18.3g

Fiesta Chicken Casserole

Prep Time: 15 minutes | Cook Time: 30 minutes | makes: 8 servings

Ingredients:

- 4 cups cubed chicken, cooked
- 1 (10- ounce) can Rotel tomatoes
- 1 cup instant rice, uncooked
- 2 cups grated Colby Jack cheese
- 1 (10 1/3 ounce) can Cream of Chicken Soup
- 2 tablespoons taco seasoning
- 2 tablespoons milk
- 1/2 cup canned corn, drained
- 1/2 cup black beans, drained
- Cilantro, chopped

Preparation:

1. Toss chicken with cheese, taco seasoning, corn, black beans, milk, and chicken soup in a bowl.
2. Spread it in a 9x9 inches baking dish, greased with cooking spray.
3. Cover it with a foil sheet and place it in the Ninja XL Pro Air Fry Oven.
4. Select the "bake" mode using the Function Keys and select Rack Level 2.
5. Set its cooking time to 30 minutes and temperature to 390 degrees F then press "START/STOP" to initiate preheating.
6. Serve warm.

Serving Suggestion: Serve the casserole with a tortilla.

Variation Tip: Add canned chickpeas to the casserole.

Nutritional Information Per Serving:

Calories 305 | Fat 25g |Sodium 532mg | Carbs 2.3g | Fiber 0.4g | Sugar 2g | Protein 18.3g

Thanksgiving Turkey

Prep Time: 15 minutes | Cook Time: 35 minutes | makes: 4 servings

Ingredients:

- 1 (2-lbs.) turkey breast
- Kosher salt, to taste
- Black pepper, to taste
- 1 teaspoon thyme, chopped
- 1 teaspoon rosemary, chopped
- 1 teaspoon sage, chopped
- 1/4 cup maple syrup
- 2 tablespoons Dijon mustard
- 1 tablespoon. butter, melted

Preparation:

1. Rub the turkey breast with maple syrup, Dijon mustard, butter, black pepper, and herbs.
2. Place the turkey in a baking tray and set it in the Ninja XL Pro Air Fry Oven.
3. Select the "Air fry" Mode using the Function Keys and select Rack Level 2.
4. Set its cooking time to 35 minutes and temperature to 390 degrees F then press "START/STOP" to initiate preheating.
5. Serve warm.

Serving Suggestion: Serve the turkey with mashed potatoes.

Variation Tip: Use cranberry preserve to season the turkey.

Nutritional Information Per Serving:

Calories 305 | Fat 25g |Sodium 532mg | Carbs 2.3g | Fiber 0.4g | Sugar 2g | Protein 18.3g

Chicken Casserole

Prep Time: 15 minutes | Cook Time: 65 minutes | makes: 8 servings

Ingredients:

- 1/4 teaspoon salt
- 1/2 teaspoon sugar
- 3 dashes black pepper
- 1 tablespoon Ranch dressing
- ¼ cup heavy whipping cream
- 2 medium potatoes, peeled and diced
- 8 oz. boneless chicken breast, cut into cubes
- 2 bacon strips, cut into pieces
- 4 tablespoons unsalted butter, cut into small pieces
- 1 cup cheddar cheese, shredded
- 1 stalk scallion, green part only, sliced

Preparation:

1. Beat ranch dressing, pepper, salt, and sugar in a bowl.
2. Grease a 9x9 inch baking pan and layer with potatoes and chicken.
3. Spread butter, bacon, cheese, scallions, and ranch mixture on top.
4. Cover with a foil sheet and place in the Ninja XL Pro Air Fry Oven.
5. Select the "bake" mode using the Function Keys and select Rack Level 2.
6. Set its cooking time to 45 minutes and temperature to 350 degrees F then press "START/STOP" to initiate preheating.
7. Remove the foil sheet and bake for another 20 minutes in the Ninja XL Pro Air Fry Oven.
8. Serve warm.

Serving Suggestion: Serve the casserole with toasted bread slices.

Variation Tip: Add boiled pasta to the chicken casserole.

Nutritional Information Per Serving:

Calories 305 | Fat 25g |Sodium 532mg | Carbs 2.3g | Fiber 0.4g | Sugar 2g | Protein 18.3g

Hash brown casserole

Prep Time: 15 minutes | Cook Time: 35 minutes | makes: 8 servings

Ingredients:

- 3 cups cauliflower, cooked and chopped
- 4 cups frozen potatoes, shredded
- 1 (10 ½ oz) can reduced-fat cream of chicken
- 1 ½ cups plain nonfat Greek yogurt
- 1 onion, diced
- Salt and black pepper to taste
- ¼ cup of sharp cheese. shredded
- 1 cup sharp cheese, shredded

Preparation:

1. Mix cauliflower with potato shreds, cream of chicken, salt, black pepper, ¼ cup cheese, onion, and yogurt in a bowl.
2. Spread this mixture in a 9x13 inches casserole dish and top it with remaining cheese.
3. Set this dish in the Ninja XL Pro Air Fry Oven.
4. Select the "bake" mode using the Function Keys and select Rack Level 2.
5. Set its cooking time to 35 minutes and temperature to 320 degrees F then press "START/STOP" to initiate preheating.
6. Serve warm.

Serving Suggestion: Serve the casserole with toasted bread slices.

Variation Tip: Add crumbled bacon on top.

Nutritional Information Per Serving:
Calories 305 | Fat 25g |Sodium 532mg | Carbs 2.3g | Fiber 0.4g | Sugar 2g | Protein 18.3g

Ground Beef Casserole

Prep Time: 15 minutes | Cook Time: 35 minutes | makes: 8 servings

Ingredients:

- 1 tablespoon vegetable oil
- 1/2 cup red onions, diced
- 2 teaspoons garlic, minced
- 1/2 cup red bell peppers, diced
- 1 lb. ground beef
- 1 tablespoon Worcestershire sauce
- 14 ½ ounces petite tomatoes, diced
- 6 oz tomato paste
- ½ teaspoon onion powder
- ½ teaspoon garlic powder
- 2 1/8 teaspoons seasoning salt

Shredded Cheese

- 1 cup Colby jack cheese, shredded
- 1 cup sharp cheese, shredded
- 1 3/4 cup mozzarella, shredded

Preparation:

1. Sauté onions and bell peppers with vegetable oil in a skillet for 2 minutes.
2. Add garlic and sauté for 20 seconds, then add ground beef.
3. Sauté until brown, then add tomatoes, tomato paste, Worcestershire sauce, garlic powder, salt, and onion powder, then mix well.
4. Transfer this beef mixture to a casserole dish, and top it with cheese.
5. Place the dish in the Ninja XL Pro Air Fry Oven.
6. Select the "bake" mode using the Function Keys and select Rack Level 2.
7. Set its cooking time to 30 minutes and temperature to 350 degrees F then press "START/STOP" to initiate preheating.
8. Serve warm.

Serving Suggestion: Serve the casserole with toasted bread slices.

Variation Tip: Add peas and corns to the casserole.

Nutritional Information Per Serving:

Calories 305 | Fat 25g |Sodium 532mg | Carbs 2.3g | Fiber 0.4g | Sugar 2g | Protein 18.3g

Air Fried Pizza

Prep Time: 15 minutes | Cook Time: 12 minutes | makes: 6 servings

Ingredients:

- 1 (8-ounces) package pizza dough
- ½ tablespoons olive oil
- 1/4 cup crushed tomatoes
- ½ garlic clove, minced
- 1/4 teaspoon oregano
- Kosher salt, to taste
- Black pepper, to taste
- 1/4 (8-ounces) mozzarella ball, cut into ¼" slices
- Basil leaves, for serving

Preparation:

1. Spread the pizza dough into an 8-inch pizza pan.
2. Brush it with olive oil, and top it with tomatoes.
3. Drizzle garlic, oregano, salt, black pepper, and Mozzarella on top.
4. Set the pizza in the Ninja XL Pro Air Fry Oven.
5. Select the "Pizza" Mode using the Function Keys and select Rack Level 2.
6. Set its cooking time to 12 minutes and temperature to 400 degrees F then press "START/STOP" to initiate preheating.
7. Serve warm.

Serving Suggestion: Serve the pizza with tomato ketchup or hot sauce.

Variation Tip: Add sliced jalapenos on top.

Nutritional Information Per Serving:
Calories 305 | Fat 25g |Sodium 532mg | Carbs 2.3g | Fiber 0.4g | Sugar 2g | Protein 18.3g

Chicken Sheet Bake

Prep Time: 15 minutes | Cook Time: 1 hr. 30 minutes | makes: 8 servings

Ingredients:

- ¼ cup olive oil
- 1 teaspoon fine grind sea salt
- ½ teaspoons pepper
- 12 ounces red potatoes
- 2 medium zucchinis, sliced
- 1 medium yellow squash, sliced
- 1 red onion, sliced
- 1 bulb garlic, chopped
- 16 ounces chicken breast
- 8 sprigs rosemary fresh
- 3 lemons, sliced

Preparation:

1. Slice the red potatoes into quarters and place them in a baking tray.
2. Drizzle black pepper, salt, and olive oil on top.
3. Set the potatoes in the Ninja XL Pro Air Fry Oven and close the lid.
4. Select the "Air Fry" Mode using the Function Keys and select Rack Level 2.
5. Set its cooking time to 10 minutes and temperature to 450 degrees F then press "START/STOP" to initiate preheating.
6. Rub the chicken breast with black pepper, salt, and add to the potatoes.
7. Spread zucchini, squash, and onion around the chicken.
8. Place the lemon slices, garlic, and rosemary on top.
9. Return the baking tray to the Air Fry Oven.
10. Select the "Air Fry" Mode using the Function Keys and select Rack Level 2.
11. Set its cooking time to 30 minutes and temperature to 325 degrees F then press "START/STOP" to initiate preheating.
12. Serve warm.

Serving Suggestion: Serve the chicken with toasted bread slices.

Variation Tip: Add corn kernels to the mixture.

Nutritional Information Per Serving:

Calories 305 | Fat 25g |Sodium 532mg | Carbs 2.3g | Fiber 0.4g | Sugar 2g | Protein 18.3g

Meatball Casserole

Prep Time: 15 minutes | Cook Time: 35 minutes | makes: 8 servings

Ingredients:

* 1-pound ground beef
* 1/2 cup mozzarella cheese, shredded
* 1/4 cup Parmesan cheese, shredded
* 1 large egg
* 1/2 cup onion, chopped
* 1 teaspoon garlic powder
* 1/2 teaspoon Italian seasoning
* 1/4 teaspoon salt
* 1/2 teaspoon black pepper
* 24 ounces pasta sauce
* 1/3 cup mozzarella cheese, shredded

Preparation:

1. Mix beef with onion, garlic powder, egg, parmesan, Italian seasoning, black pepper, and salt in a bowl.
2. Make golf-ball sized meatballs out of this mixture and spread them in a casserole dish.
3. Set the dish in the Ninja XL Pro Air Fry Oven to bake the meatballs.
4. Select the "bake" mode using the Function Keys and select Rack Level 2.
5. Set its cooking time to 20 minutes and temperature to 400 degrees F then press "START/STOP" to initiate preheating.
6. Top the baked meatballs with the pasta sauce and mozzarella cheese.
7. Bake again for 15 minutes in the Ninja XL Pro Air Fry Oven.
8. Serve warm.

Serving Suggestion: Serve the meatball casserole with boiled spaghetti.

Variation Tip: Add toasted croutons on top.

Nutritional Information Per Serving:
Calories 305 | Fat 25g |Sodium 532mg | Carbs 2.3g | Fiber 0.4g | Sugar 2g | Protein 18.3g

Turkey breast

Prep Time: 15 minutes | Cook Time: 60 minutes | makes: 6 servings

Ingredients:

- 3 lbs. boneless breast
- ¼ cup mayonnaise
- 2 teaspoons poultry seasoning
- 1 teaspoon salt
- ½ teaspoons garlic powder
- ¼ teaspoons black pepper

Preparation:

1. Mix mayonnaise, poultry seasoning, black pepper, garlic powder, and salt in a bowl.
2. Rub this mixture over the turkey breast and set in a baking tray.
3. Set this baking tray in the Ninja XL Pro Air Fry Oven.
4. Select the "Air Fry" Mode using the Function Keys and select Rack Level 2.
5. Set its cooking time to 60 minutes and temperature to 360 degrees F then press "START/STOP" to initiate preheating.
6. Flip the turkey once cooked halfway through.
7. Serve warm.

Serving Suggestion: Serve the turkey with a maple glaze on top.

Variation Tip: Brush with barbecue sauce before cooking.

Nutritional Information Per Serving:

Calories 305 | Fat 25g |Sodium 532mg | Carbs 2.3g | Fiber 0.4g | Sugar 2g | Protein 18.3g

Roasted Chicken

Prep Time: 15 minutes | Cook Time: 50 minutes | makes: 10 servings

Ingredients:

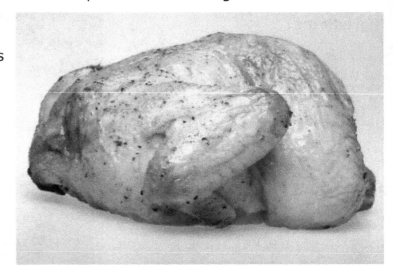

- 1 (5 lb.) whole chicken, giblets removed
- 2 tablespoons avocado oil
- 1 tablespoon kosher salt
- 1 teaspoon black pepper
- 1 teaspoon garlic powder
- 1 teaspoon paprika
- 1/2 teaspoon dried basil
- 1/2 teaspoon dried oregano
- 1/2 teaspoon dried thyme

Preparation:

1. Rub the chicken with avocado oil, salt, black pepper, garlic powder, paprika, basil, oregano, and thyme.
2. Place the seasoned chicken in a baking tray.
3. Set the baking tray in the Ninja XL Pro Air Fry Oven and close its door.
4. Select the "Whole Roast" Mode using the Function Keys and select Rack Level 2.
5. Set its cooking time to 50 minutes and temperature to 360 degrees F then press "START/STOP" to initiate preheating.
6. Flip the whole chicken and cook for another 10 minutes.
7. Serve warm.

Serving Suggestion: Serve the chicken with roasted veggies.

Variation Tip: Stuff the chicken with garlic, onion, and celery.

Nutritional Information Per Serving:

Calories 305 | Fat 25g |Sodium 532mg | Carbs 2.3g | Fiber 0.4g | Sugar 2g | Protein 18.3g

Chapter 7: Vegetables and Sides

Vegetables Mix

Prep Time: 15 minutes | Cook Time: 20 minutes | makes: 6 servings

Ingredients:

- 4 ounces mushrooms, sliced
- 1 yellow summer squash, sliced
- 1 zucchini, sliced
- 1 red bell pepper, seeded and sliced
- 1/2 sweet onion, sliced
- 1 tablespoon olive oil
- Salt and black pepper to taste

Preparation:

1. Toss the red bell pepper, zucchini, summer squash, mushrooms, and onion in a large bowl.
2. Stir in black pepper, salt, and olive oil to season the veggies.
3. Spread these vegetables in a baking pan evenly.
4. Transfer these veggies to the Ninja XL Pro Air Fry Oven and close its door.
5. Select the "Bake" Mode using the Function Keys and select Rack Level 2.
6. Set its cooking time to 10 minutes and temperature to 350 degrees F then press "START/STOP" to initiate preheating.
7. Serve warm.

Serving Suggestion: Serve the veggies with boiled rice and tomato sauce.

Variation Tip: Add crushed tomatoes for a saucy texture.

Nutritional Information Per Serving:

Calories 191 | Fat 2.2g |Sodium 276mg | Carbs 7.7g | Fiber 0.9g | Sugar 1.4g | Protein 8.8g

Brussels Sprouts Gratin

Prep Time: 15 minutes | Cook Time: 30 minutes | makes: 8 servings

Ingredients:

- 1 lb. Brussels sprouts
- 1 garlic clove, cut in half
- 3 tablespoons butter, divided
- 2 tablespoons shallots, minced
- 2 tablespoons all-purpose flour
- Salt, to taste
- Black pepper
- 1 dash ground nutmeg
- 1 cup milk
- 1/2 cup fontina cheese, shredded
- 1 strip of bacon, cooked and crumbled

- 1/2 cup fine bread crumbs

Preparation:

1. Trim the Brussels sprouts and remove their outer leaves.
2. Slice the sprouts into quarters, then rinse them under cold water.
3. Grease a gratin dish with cooking spray and rub it with garlic halves.
4. Boil salted water in a suitable pan, then add Brussels sprouts.
5. Cook the sprouts for 3 minutes, then immediately drain.
6. Place a suitable saucepan over medium-low heat and melt 2 tablespoons butter in it.
7. Toss in shallots and sauté until soft, then stir in flour, nutmeg, ½ teaspoons salt, and black pepper.
8. Stir cook for 2 minutes, then gradually add milk and a half and half cream.
9. Mix well and add bacon along with shredded cheese.
10. Fold in brussels sprouts and transfer this mixture to the casserole dish.
11. Toss breadcrumbs with 1 tablespoon butter and spread over the casserole.
12. Transfer the Brussels sprouts casserole to the Ninja XL Pro Air Fry Oven and close its door.
13. Select the "bake" mode using the Function Keys and select Rack Level 2.
14. Set its cooking time to 25 minutes and temperature to 350 degrees F then press "START/STOP" to initiate preheating.
15. Enjoy!

Serving Suggestion: Serve the gratin with toasted bread slices.

Variation Tip: Use crushed cornflakes for a more crispy texture.

Nutritional Information Per Serving:

Calories 378 | Fat 3.8g |Sodium 620mg | Carbs 13.3g | Fiber 2.4g | Sugar 1.2g | Protein 5.4g

Mayo Broccoli Casserole

Prep Time: 15 minutes | Cook Time: 45 minutes | makes: 6 servings

Ingredients:

- 1 cup mayonnaise
- 10 ½ ounces cream of celery soup
- 2 large eggs, beaten
- 20 ounces broccoli, chopped
- 2 tablespoons onion, minced
- 1 cup Cheddar cheese, grated
- 1 tablespoon Worcestershire sauce
- 1 teaspoon seasoned salt
- Black pepper, to taste
- 2 tablespoons butter

Preparation:

1. Whisk mayonnaise with eggs, condensed soup in a large bowl.
2. Stir in salt, black pepper, Worcestershire sauce, and cheddar cheese.
3. Spread broccoli and onion in a greased casserole dish.
4. Top the veggies with the mayonnaise mixture.
5. Transfer this broccoli casserole to the Ninja XL Pro Air Fry Oven and Close its door.
6. Select the "bake" mode using the Function Keys and select Rack Level 2.
7. Set its cooking time to 45 minutes and temperature to 350 degrees F then press "START/STOP" to initiate preheating.
8. Slice and serve warm.

Serving Suggestion: Serve the casserole with toasted bread slices.

Variation Tip: Add chopped celery sticks to the mixture.

Nutritional Information Per Serving:

Calories 341 | Fat 4g |Sodium 547mg | Carbs 36.4g | Fiber 1.2g | Sugar 1g | Protein 10.3g

Green Bean Casserole

Prep Time: 15 minutes | Cook Time: 25 minutes | makes: 6 servings

Ingredients:

- 4 cups green beans, cooked and chopped
- 3 tablespoons butter
- 8 ounces mushrooms, sliced
- ¼ cup onion, chopped
- 2 tablespoons flour
- 1 teaspoon salt
- ¼ teaspoon ground black pepper
- 1 ½ cups milk
- 2 cups cheddar cheese, shredded
- 2 tablespoons sour cream
- 1 cup soft breadcrumbs
- 2 tablespoons butter, melted
- ¼ cup Parmesan cheese, grated
- 1 cup French fried onions

Preparation:

1. Add butter to a suitable saucepan and melt it over medium-low heat.
2. Toss in onion and mushrooms, then sauté until soft.
3. Stir in flour, salt, and black. Mix well, then slowly pour in the milk.
4. Stir in sour cream, green beans, and cheddar cheese, then cook until it thickens.
5. Transfer this green bean mixture to a casserole dish and spread it evenly.
6. Toss breadcrumbs with fried onion and butter.
7. Top the casserole with this breadcrumb's mixture.
8. Transfer the vegetable cream casserole to the Ninja XL Pro Air Fry Oven and close its door.
9. Select the "bake" mode using the Function Keys and select Rack Level 2.
10. Set its cooking time to 25 minutes and temperature to 350 degrees F then press "START/STOP" to initiate preheating.
11. Serve and enjoy!

Serving Suggestion: Serve the casserole with mashed potatoes.

Variation Tip: Add crispy dried onion for better taste.

Nutritional Information Per Serving:
Calories 304 | Fat 31g |Sodium 834mg | Carbs 21.4g | Fiber 0.2g | Sugar 0.3g | Protein 4.6g

Vegetable Casserole

Prep Time: 15 minutes | Cook Time: 45 minutes | makes: 6 servings

Ingredients:

- 2 cups peas
- 8 ounces mushrooms, sliced
- 4 tablespoons all-purpose flour
- 1 ½ cups celery, sliced
- 1 ½ cups carrots, sliced
- ½ teaspoon mustard powder
- 2 cups of milk
- Salt and black pepper, to taste
- 7 tablespoons butter
- 1 cup breadcrumbs
- ½ cup Parmesan cheese, grated

Preparation:

1. Grease and rub a casserole dish with butter and keep it aside.
2. Add carrots, onion, and celery to a saucepan, then fill it with water.
3. Cover this pot and cook for 10 minutes, then stir in peas.
4. Cook for 4 minutes, then strain the vegetables.
5. Now melt 1 tablespoon butter in the same saucepan and toss in mushrooms to sauté.
6. Once the mushrooms are soft, transfer them to the vegetables.
7. Prepare the sauce by melting 4 tablespoons butter in a saucepan.
8. Stir in mustard and flour, then stir cook for 2 minutes.
9. Gradually pour in the milk and stir cook until thickened, then add salt and black pepper.
10. Add vegetables and mushrooms to the flour milk mixture and mix well to blend.
11. Spread this vegetable blend in the casserole dish evenly.
12. Toss the breadcrumbs with the remaining butter and spread it on top of the vegetables.
13. Top this casserole dish with cheese.
14. Transfer the vegetable casserole to the Ninja XL Pro Air Fry Oven and close its door.
15. Select the "bake" mode using the Function Keys and select Rack Level 2.
16. Set its cooking time to 25 minutes and temperature to 350 degrees F then press "START/STOP" to initiate preheating.
17. Serve warm.

Serving Suggestion: Serve the casserole with toasted bread slices.

Variation Tip: Add toasted croutons on top.

Nutritional Information Per Serving:

Calories 338 | Fat 24g |Sodium 620mg | Carbs 58.3g | Fiber 2.4g | Sugar 1.2g | Protein 5.4g

Mushroom Skewers

Prep Time: 15 minutes | Cook Time: 7 minutes | makes: 6 servings

Ingredients:

- 1/4 cup balsamic vinegar
- 2 tablespoons soy sauce
- 2 garlic cloves, minced
- Black pepper
- 1 lb. cremini mushrooms, sliced 1/2" thick

Preparation:

1. Toss mushrooms with vinegar, soy sauce, garlic, and black pepper.
2. Thread them on the mini wooden skewers.
3. Set the skewers in the baking tray and transfer to the Air Fry Oven.
4. Select the "Air Fry" Mode using the Function Keys and select Rack Level 2.
5. Set its cooking time to 7 minutes and temperature to 350 degrees F then press "START/STOP" to initiate preheating.
6. Serve warm.

Serving Suggestion: Serve the mushrooms with barbecue sauce.

Variation Tip: Add paprika for more spice.

Nutritional Information Per Serving:

Calories 324 | Fat 5g |Sodium 432mg | Carbs 13.1g | Fiber 0.3g | Sugar 1g | Protein 5.7g

Sweet Potato Casserole

Prep Time: 15 minutes | Cook Time: 35 minutes | makes: 8 servings

Ingredients:

- 3 cups brown sugar, packed
- 1 ½ cup butter, melted
- 4 large eggs, beaten
- 2 teaspoons vanilla extract
- 1 cup milk
- 6 cups sweet potatoes, boiled and mashed
- 2/3 cup flour
- 8 ounces pecans, chopped

Preparation:

1. Mix the sweet potato mash with vanilla extract, milk, eggs, 2 ½ brown sugar, and 1 cup melted butter in a large bowl.
2. Spread this sweet potato mixture in a casserole dish.
3. Now whisk remaining sugar and butter with flour in a separate bowl.
4. Fold in pecan, then top the sweet potatoes mixed with this pecan mixture.
5. Transfer the sweet potato casserole to the Ninja XL Pro Air Fry Oven and close its door.
6. Select the "bake" mode using the Function Keys and select Rack Level 2.
7. Set its cooking time to 35 minutes and temperature to 350 degrees F then press "START/STOP" to initiate preheating.
8. Slice and serve!

Serving Suggestion: Serve the casserole with toasted bread slices.

Variation Tip: Ground chicken or beef can also be used instead of ground sausage.

Nutritional Information Per Serving:

Calories 421 | Fat 10.1g |Sodium 380mg | Carbs 25.3g | Fiber 2.4g | Sugar 1.2g | Protein 2.1g

Cauliflower Broccoli Medley

Prep Time: 15 minutes | Cook Time: 8 minutes | makes: 2 servings

Ingredients:

- 1/2 lb. broccoli, florets
- 1/2 lb. cauliflower, florets
- 1 tablespoon olive oil
- Black pepper, to taste
- Salt, to taste

Preparation:

1. Toss all the veggies with seasoning in a large bowl.
2. Spread these vegetables in the Air Fryer basket.
3. Place the veggies inside the Ninja XL Pro Air Fry Oven and close its door.
4. Select the "Air Fry" Mode using the Function Keys and select Rack Level 2.
5. Set its cooking time to 8 minutes and temperature to 400 degrees F then press "START/STOP" to initiate preheating.
6. Serve warm.

Serving Suggestion: Serve the veggies with spaghetti squash.

Variation Tip: Add paprika for more spice.

Nutritional Information Per Serving:

Calories 118 | Fat 5.7g |Sodium 124mg | Carbs 7g | Fiber 0.1g | Sugar 0.3g | Protein 4.9g

Italian Baked Vegetables

Prep Time: 15 minutes | Cook Time: 15 minutes | makes: 4 servings

Ingredients:

- 2 bell peppers cored, chopped
- 2 carrots, peeled and sliced
- 1 zucchini, ends trimmed, sliced
- 1 broccoli, florets
- ½ red onion, peeled and diced
- 2 tablespoons olive oil
- 1 ½ teaspoon Italian seasoning
- 2 garlic cloves, minced
- Salt and Black pepper, to taste
- 1 cup grape tomatoes
- 1 tablespoon fresh lemon juice

Preparation:

1. Toss all the veggies with olive oil, Italian seasoning, salt, black pepper, and garlic in a large salad bowl.
2. Spread this broccoli-zucchini mixture in the Ninja baking pan.
3. Transfer the baking pan to the Ninja XL Pro Air Fry Oven and close its door.
4. Select the "bake" mode using the Function Keys and select Rack Level 2.
5. Set its cooking time to 15 minutes and temperature to 400 degrees F then press "START/STOP" to initiate preheating.
6. Serve warm with lemon juice on top.
7. Enjoy.

Serving Suggestion: Serve the veggies as a pizza topping.

Variation Tip: Add olives or sliced mushrooms.

Nutritional Information Per Serving:

Calories 246 | Fat 15g |Sodium 220mg | Carbs 40.3g | Fiber 2.4g | Sugar 1.2g | Protein 12.4g

Chapter 8: Dessert Recipes

Chocolate Cake

Prep Time: 15 minutes | Cook Time: 15 minutes | makes: 8 servings

Ingredients:

- ¼ cup white sugar
- 3 ½ tablespoons butter, softened
- 1 egg
- 1 tablespoon apricot jam
- 6 tablespoons all-purpose flour
- 1 tablespoon cocoa powder
- Cooking spray
- Salt to taste
- Heavy cream, to serve

Preparation:

1. Beat butter, sugar, egg, and jam in a bowl until creamy.
2. Stir in cocoa powder, salt, and flour, then mix until smooth.
3. Spread this batter in a greased fluted tube pan.
4. Place this pan in the Ninja XL Pro Air Fry Oven and close the lid.
5. Select the "bake" mode using the Function Keys and select Rack Level 2.
6. Set its cooking time to 15 minutes and temperature to 325 degrees F then press "START/STOP" to initiate preheating.
7. Allow the cake to cool, then slice.
8. Garnish with cream.
9. Serve.

Serving Suggestion: Serve the cakes with sprinkles and cream on top.

Variation Tip: Add chopped nuts to the batter.

Nutritional Information Per Serving:
Calories 248 | Fat 16g |Sodium 95mg | Carbs 38.4g | Fiber 0.3g | Sugar 10g | Protein 14.1g

Strawberry Roll Cake

Prep Time: 15 minutes | Cook Time: 12 minutes | makes: 6 servings

Ingredients:

Sponge Cake

- ½ cup of sugar
- 4 large eggs
- ¾ cup all-purpose flour
- 1 teaspoon vanilla extract

Filling:

- ½ cup heavy whipping cream
- 1 cup butter salted
- 1 cup confectioner sugar
- 2 teaspoons vanilla extract
- 8 ounces strawberry preserves

Preparation:

1. Beat sugar with 4 eggs in a mixing bowl with an electric mixer for 5 minutes.
2. Stir in vanilla and flour, then mix until smooth.
3. Spread this sponge cake batter in a 13x13 baking pan, lined with parchment paper.
4. Place the cake pan in the Ninja XL Pro Air Fry Oven and close its door.
5. Select the "Bake" Mode using the Function Keys and select Rack Level 2.
6. Set its cooking time to 12 minutes and temperature to 325 degrees F then press "START/STOP" to initiate preheating.
7. Meanwhile, beat cream with butter, vanilla, and sugar in a bowl on medium-high speed until smooth.
8. Place the sponge cake along with the parchment paper on the working surface, top it with buttercream.
9. Add strawberry preserves on top evenly, then roll the cake gently.
10. Slice and serve.

Serving Suggestion: Serve the cake slices with strawberry sauce or jam.

Variation Tip: Use blueberry or cranberry preserve for a change of flavor

Nutritional Information Per Serving:

Calories 245 | Fat 14g |Sodium 122mg | Carbs 23.3g | Fiber 1.2g | Sugar 12g | Protein 4.3g

Fudgy Brownies

Prep Time: 15 minutes | Cook Time: 35 minutes | makes: 8 servings

Ingredients:

- ¾ cup butter salted
- 1¾ cup dark chocolate chips
- 1 teaspoon espresso powder
- ¾ teaspoons sea salt
- 1½ cups sugar
- 5 large eggs
- ⅓ cup vegetable oil
- 2 teaspoons vanilla extract
- ½ cup unsweetened cocoa powder
- 1½ cups all-purpose flour

Preparation:

1. Add melted butter and 1 cup chocolate chips to a bowl and heat for 2 minutes in the microwave until melted.
2. Mix well, then add 1 teaspoon espresso powder, then stir well.
3. Beat eggs, sugar, salt, vanilla extract, oil, and chocolate mixture in a bowl for 5 seconds.
4. Stir in cocoa powder and flour, then mix until smooth.
5. Add ¾ chocolate chips, then mix with a spatula.
6. Layer an 11 ½ x 9 inches baking pan with parchment pan.
7. Spread the prepared batter in the pan and place it in the Ninja XL Pro Air Fry Oven.
8. Select the "Bake" Mode using the Function Keys and select Rack Level 2.
9. Set its cooking time to 35 minutes and temperature to 325 degrees F then press "START/STOP" to initiate preheating.
10. Allow the cake to cool, then slice.
11. Serve.

Serving Suggestion: Serve the brownies with a scoop of ice cream.

Variation Tip: Add chopped nuts to the batter.

Nutritional Information Per Serving:

Calories 271 | Fat 15g |Sodium 108mg | Carbs 33g | Fiber 1g | Sugar 26g | Protein 4g

Cherry Eggrolls

Prep Time: 15 minutes | Cook Time: 5 minutes | makes: 8 servings

Ingredients:

- ½ 8 ounces package cream cheese, softened
- ⅓ cup cherry jam
- ¼ cup dried red cherries, chopped
- 16 wonton wrappers
- 1 tablespoon butter, melted
- 3 tablespoons sugar
- ½ teaspoon ground cinnamon

Preparation:

1. Beat cream cheese and cherry jam in a bowl.
2. Stir in dried cherries and refrigerate the mixture for 30 minutes.
3. Spread the wonton wrappers on the working surface.
4. Wet the edges of the wrappers with water.
5. Add a teaspoon of cherry mixture at the center of the wrapper.
6. Fold the two sides of each wrapper and roll these wraps.
7. Place the rolls in the Air fryer basket, spray with cooking oil.
8. Set the basket in the Ninja XL Pro Air Fry Oven and close the lid.
9. Select the "Air Fry" Mode using the Function Keys and select Rack Level 2.
10. Set its cooking time to 5 minutes and temperature to 360 degrees F then press "START/STOP" to initiate preheating.
11. Drizzle cinnamon and sugar on top and serve.

Serving Suggestion: Serve the rolls with sweet cream cheese dip.

Variation Tip: Use strawberry jam instead of cherry jam.

Nutritional Information Per Serving:

Calories 327 | Fat 31g |Sodium 86mg | Carbs 49g | Fiber 1.8g | Sugar 12g | Protein 13.5g

Pear Pies

Prep Time: 15 minutes | Cook Time: 14 minutes | makes: 8 servings

Ingredients:

- 4 tablespoons butter
- 6 tablespoons brown sugar
- 1 teaspoon ground cinnamon
- 2 medium pears, peeled and diced
- 1 teaspoon cornstarch
- 2 teaspoons cold water
- 9-inch double-crust pie
- Cooking spray
- ½ tablespoon grapeseed oil
- ¼ cup powdered sugar
- 1 teaspoon milk

Preparation:

1. Sauté pears with butter, cinnamon, and brown sugar in a skillet for 5 minutes.
2. Whisk cornstarch with cold water and pour it into the egg mixture.
3. Stir and cook this mixture for 1 minute until it thickens.
4. Spread the pie crust on a floured surface and cut the dough into 8 rectangles.
5. Divide the filling on top of all the rectangles, then fold in half.
6. Crimp the edges with a fork and cut 4 slits on top.
7. Place the pear pies in the air fryer basket and brush them with grapeseed oil.
8. Set the Air fryer basket in the Ninja XL Pro Air Fry Oven.
9. Select the "bake" mode using the Function Keys and select Rack Level 2.
10. Set its cooking time to 8 minutes and temperature to 385 degrees F then press "START/STOP" to initiate preheating.
11. Mix sugar with milk in a small bowl and brush this mixture on top.
12. Serve.

Serving Suggestion: Serve the pies with mixed fruit jam.

Variation Tip: Add peaches to the fillings.

Nutritional Information Per Serving:

Calories 318 | Fat 20g |Sodium 192mg | Carbs 23.7g | Fiber 0.9g | Sugar 19g | Protein 5.2g

Cherry Crumble

Prep Time: 15 minutes | Cook Time: 25 minutes | makes: 8 servings

Ingredients:

- ⅓ cup butter, crumbled
- 3 cups pitted cherries
- 10 tablespoons white sugar
- 2 teaspoons lemon juice
- 1 cup all-purpose baking flour
- 1 teaspoon vanilla powder
- 1 teaspoon ground nutmeg
- 1 teaspoon ground cinnamon

Preparation:

1. Toss pitted cherries with lemon juice and 2 tablespoons sugar in a bowl.
2. Spread the cherries mixture in an 8 inches baking dish.
3. Whisk flour, butter, and 6 tablespoons sugar in a bowl.
4. Spread this flour mixture on top of the cherries.
5. Mix vanilla powder, nutmeg, cinnamon, and 2 tablespoons sugar in a bowl
6. Drizzle this cinnamon mixture on top of the flour mixture.
7. Select the "bake" mode using the Function Keys and select Rack Level 2.
8. Set its cooking time to 25 minutes and temperature to 325 degrees F then press "START/STOP" to initiate preheating.
9. Serve.

Serving Suggestion: Serve the crumble with fresh berries on top.

Variation Tip: Add blueberry preserves to the filling.

Nutritional Information Per Serving:

Calories 295 | Fat 3g |Sodium 355mg | Carbs 10g | Fiber 1g | Sugar 5g | Protein 1g

Pecan Apples

Prep Time: 15 minutes | Cook Time: 15 minutes | makes: 4 servings

Ingredients:

- 2 medium apples, top cut and cored
- 1 tablespoon butter, melted
- 2 tablespoons pecans, chopped
- 1 tablespoon brown sugar
- 1 teaspoon all-purpose flour
- ¼ teaspoon apple pie spice
- Vanilla ice cream or yogurt

Preparation:

1. Mix pecans, butter, brown sugar, apple pie spices, and flour in a small bowl.
2. Place the apple in the Air fryer basket, and stuff pecans mixture in it, then place the cut top to cover.
3. Return the basket to the Air Fry Oven.
4. Select the "Air Fry" Mode using the Function Keys and select Rack Level 2.
5. Set its cooking time to 15 minutes and temperature to 360 degrees F then press "START/STOP" to initiate preheating.
6. Serve.

Serving Suggestion: Serve with caramel sauce or chocolate syrup on top.

Variation Tip: Add walnuts to the filling.

Nutritional Information Per Serving:
Calories 398 | Fat 14g |Sodium 272mg | Carbs 34g | Fiber 1g | Sugar 9.3g | Protein 1.3g

Apple Pies

Prep Time: 15 minutes | Cook Time: 7 minutes | makes: 10 servings

Ingredients:

- 1 (14 ounces) package refrigerated pie crusts
- 1 (21 ounces) can apple pie filling
- 1 egg, beaten
- 2 tablespoons cinnamon sugar
- Cooking spray

Preparation:

1. Spread each pie crust on a lightly floured surface and cut ten 2 ¼ inches circles out of each using a cookie cutter to get 20 circles in total.
2. Divide the apple pie filling into the top 10 circles.
3. Top the filling with the remaining circles on top and crimp the edges with a fork.
4. Brush the pies with beaten eggs and drizzle cinnamon sugar on top.
5. Set the pies in the Air fryer basket and set the basket in the Ninja XL Pro Air Fry Oven.
6. Select the "bake" mode using the Function Keys and select Rack Level 2.
7. Set its cooking time to 7 minutes and temperature to 360 degrees F then press "START/STOP" to initiate preheating.
8. Serve.

Serving Suggestion: Serve the pies with apple sauce.

Variation Tip: Add apple sauce to the filling.

Nutritional Information Per Serving:

Calories 317 | Fat 12g |Sodium 79mg | Carbs 14.8g | Fiber 1.1g | Sugar 8g | Protein 5g

Butter Cake

Prep Time: 15 minutes | Cook Time: 15 minutes | makes: 6 servings

Ingredients:

- 7 tablespoons butter
- ¼ cup brown sugar
- 2 tablespoons white sugar
- 1 egg
- 1 ⅔ cups all-purpose flour
- 1 pinch salt
- Cooking spray
- 6 tablespoons milk

Preparation:

1. Grease a fluted tube pan with cooking oil or spray.
2. Beat brown sugar, sugar with butter in a bowl using an electric mixer.
3. Stir in salt, milk, and flour, then mix until smooth.
4. Pour the chocolate batter into a greased tube pan and place it in the Ninja XL Pro Air Fry Oven.
5. Select the "Bake" Mode using the Function Keys and select Rack Level 2.
6. Set its cooking time to 15 minutes and temperature to 350 degrees F then press "START/STOP" to initiate preheating.
7. Allow the baked cake to cool and then remove from the pan.
8. Slice and serve.

Serving Suggestion: Serve the cake with chocolate syrup on top.

Variation Tip: Add vanilla extracts to the batter.

Nutritional Information Per Serving:
Calories 253 | Fat 8.9g |Sodium 340mg | Carbs 24.7g | Fiber 1.2g | Sugar 11.3g | Protein 5.3g

Conclusion

Ninja Foodi XL Pro Air Fry Oven combines all the necessary cooking operations of the day in a single unit. That has not only brought ease to the kitchen floors but also guaranteed the smart management of kitchen space. Its efficient cooking mechanism has helped professionals as well as homemakers to enhance their cooking skills. If you want to cook like expert chefs and enjoy super crispy and freshly roasted or baked meals in just a snitch, then give Ninja Foodi XL Pro Air Fry Oven a chance.

The big size of this Ninja Foodi XL Pro Air Fry Oven will solve all your cooking problems because there is nothing that this cooking unit can not cook. All you need to do is to add food of different variety according to the recipes shared in this book, set up the cooking mode, cooking time, and temperature, then wait for the beep and Voila! You will be surprised to see the results. From good texture to great taste, now you enjoy it all using your Ninja XL Pro Air Fry Oven. Before the 10 in 1 Ninja XL, I had used several other Air Fry Ovens, and none of them seemed perfect for me since I needed a unit that would offer all the cooking modes, a large capacity, along with an effective heating mechanism. But when I came across the Ninja XL pro, it offered everything that I was looking for. Creating a new menu using this appliance was less of an effort and more fun because it is so user-friendly and easy to use. The multi-level cooking provides even heat through its smart convection mechanism.

So, if you are planning to enjoy all the perks offered by this amazing appliance, then it's about time that you bring it home, set up it on your kitchen counter, and start creating some magical flavors at home. You will be amazed to know how quickly this single cooking unit changes everything in the kitchen for you. No other appliance can make cooking as convenient as the Ninja XL Pro Air Fry Oven. So, try all the air fry oven recipes from this cookbook and create a menu of your own.